deep

from surface to substance

A Collection of Daily
Readings based on Proverbs

INTRODUCTION BY
MIKE WOODRUFF

Christ Church
100 N. Waukegan Rd.
Lake Forest, IL 60045

TABLE OF CONTENTS

WEEK 4: **DEEP INSIGHT**

WEEK 5: **DEEP INTIMACY**

WEEK 6: **DEEP BONDS**

APPENDIX

FREEDIVING

Freediving was practiced in ancient cultures to gather food or harvest resources such as pearls. In its modern form, freediving is a solitary sport that relies on an underwater diver's ability to hold a single breath and to attain the deepest depth possible on that one breath. It is said among freedivers that scuba divers dive to look around, but freedivers dive to look within.

It requires a tremendous amount of training and discipline—just as our quest to gain a greater depth of character and wisdom requires training and discipline.

When diving under the water, movements slow down and surrounding sounds soften and fade. Similarly, the deeper we dive into knowing God through his Word and cultivating various spiritual disciplines, the more the frantic pace and competing noise of modern life slows and softens.

When going deep with God, we enter a languid peace with God and others, no matter the trials modern life may bring. As we learn to live, think and work with godly depth as the goal, we gain new perspective on life—life as it was meant to be lived—with God. We gain deeper insights, intimacy and bonds in our relationships with God and with others. We find substance in life that all our hurried and harried efforts to keep up can never bring.

AN INTRODUCTION TO DEEP

*The desperate need today is not for a greater number of intelligent
people, or gifted people, but for deep people.*

Richard J. Foster

*Whatever is familiar, whatever is titillating, whatever is undemanding,
whatever is immediately useful, whatever confirms my preexisting
biases, whatever provokes a sense of righteous anger and justified
outrage, if there is anything trending and if there is anything worthy of
retweeting, react briefly and superficially to these things.*[1]

Philippians 4:8, rewritten for today's culture

Things are different; consequently, so are you. In fact, you're a very different person today than you would have been if you'd been born in rural Kansas back in 1875 or grew up in the Amazon jungle today. I'm not saying the present you is better (or worse), just different.

And I am setting up a second point: it is up to you to make the most of your life, and this is true no matter when or where you were born. Life is a gift from God and we are expected to be good stewards of it.

Let me back up and get a running start.

IT'S A NEW DAY

The last fifty years have witnessed unprecedented change. During this period the West has been transformed by an explosion of technology, wealth, information and opportunity. In fact, the word *transformed* is not strong enough. We've undergone a revolution.

---

1   Philippians 4:8 actually reads: Finally, brothers and sisters, whatever is true, whatever is noble, whatever is right, whatever is pure, whatever is lovely, whatever is admirable—if anything is excellent or praiseworthy—think about such things.

If you dig into history you will see that every few hundred years the social and political landscape changes during a brief window of time. I am not talking days or weeks. The magnitude of change I am referring to usually takes forty to fifty years to play out. But during this relatively brief window so many things are altered that children born at the tail end of the change find it impossible to imagine the lives of their grandparents or the world into which their own parents were born.[2]

We've spent the last thirty years moving through one of these windows. In fact, things have been unfolding so quickly that my own children (now in their twenties) not only dismiss stories of my childhood, they are skeptical of my reports of the world into which they were born.

> *Me:* You realize that when Austin was born we did not have cell phones or home computers.
>
> *Them:* No laptops, just desktops?
>
> *Me:* No computers at all. Almost no one did. They were too big and expensive. When I took a computer class in college, the computer filled an entire room, it cost hundreds of thousands of dollars and it didn't do much. More shocking still, the only "computer game" around was "Pong," and it consisted of a single blip moving back and forth across the screen.
>
> *Them:* Nice try Dad. And gas was five cents and you walked to school uphill both ways.

It's difficult to comprehend how quickly things have changed.

And it's also challenging to know what to make of it. Clearly, in some ways things are better than before—e.g., medical care is dramatically improved, food production has been expanded, we have eradicated certain diseases, expanded civil rights and reduced extreme poverty. However, in other ways things are worse—e.g., the number of children born outside of wedlock has skyrocketed, test scores are down, sex trafficking is up and pornography is now a multi-billion dollar industry.

I could expand my list, but others have already developed each point at great

---

2   Peter Drucker develops this point in greater length in the first chapter of his 1993 book, *The Post-Capitalist Society.*

length. My goal for this introduction is pretty modest. Right now I only wish to establish three points:

- We live in a new day.

- Consequently, we are being shaped by different factors.

- The result is, we are different people.

FIVE WAYS YOUR LIFE DIFFERS FROM YOUR GREAT GRANDPARENTS'

How different is the current you from the you that you would have been if you'd been born in rural Kansas in 1875 or were growing up in the Amazon today? It's impossible to give a definitive answer to this question, but we can easily note a few things.

First: We move more quickly. If you missed the stage coach one hundred years ago, it was no big deal. You'd catch the next one, in a month. Today if we miss our section of the revolving door we feel behind, and if our laptop (smartphone, tablet or wrist watch) takes more than a half second to boot up—or isn't able to download the Library of Congress in three seconds—we act as if we may not be able to survive the inconvenience. Everywhere we look, people are *racing around, multi-tasking* and trying to *catch up.*

Second: We have more stuff. Capitalism, Madison Avenue and the tech explosion have combined in ways Adam Smith did not foresee.[3] The result is that many of us now have more stuff by the time that we are 25 than our great grandparents accumulated over their entire lives. In fact, some now have so much stuff that it no longer fits into the super-sized closets, expanded garages or dramatically larger homes that are remarkably commonplace.[4] [5]

---

3   Of course one of the reasons we have more stuff is because we have greater wealth. The average US citizen has a standard of living few could have imagined fifty years ago. To be sure, much of this has been financed with debt—but there is a lot of money out there as well.

4   A few years ago I went back to the house I grew up in and asked if I could step in and look around. It was very disorienting because my parent's bedroom—which I remember as being huge—was so small it barely fit a bed. Today many have much larger rooms and still end up renting garage-size lockers across town in order to have enough space to store all of their possessions.

5   One of the complaints I'm hearing more frequently these days comes from the adult children of men and women who passed away without cleaning out their home, thereby burdening their children with the chore of sorting through forty or fifty years of accumulated stuff.

Third: We feel busier. I am not suggesting that life is harder—after all, few of us are milking the cow, growing our food, making our clothes or even changing the oil in the car. I am saying that we feel busier. Why? It's simple: the more options we have, the more we feel the limits of time. And we have options! *What should I do after work today? Visit a friend? Hit golf balls? Exercise? Go to the PTA meeting? Volunteer at the church? Shop at the mall? Call my mom? Read a book? Check my stocks? Play* Angry Birds? *Watch TV? And if it's TV, do I really mean TV, or do I mean cable, TiVo, YouTube, HBO or Netflix?* People feel behind when they have too much to do, but they also feel behind—and busier—when they have taped seven hours of "must-see TV" but only have four hours in which to watch it. My point is not that life is harder, but that we feel busier than people in the past.

And part of both the cause and effect is that many have not only traded in the Sabbath for Sunday, but they have traded Sunday for the weekend—i.e., they have not only traded in a day God established for our restoration for a day set up for amusement; but they have given up a day of amusement for another day of catching up.

Fourth: We face more distractions and temptations. The number of people trying to grab our attention—almost always so they can sell us something that we do not need—now numbers in the tens of millions. Pause to think about this for a moment. Thousands of very smart people woke up this morning intent on getting you to buy something. And because you have started looking past their previous methods of attracting your attention—e.g., newspaper fliers, radio jingles and highway billboards—they have moved on to new approaches: TV screens at the grocery store and gas pump, banner ads on websites and stickers on fruit. And now that we have computers powerful enough to crunch unimaginable amounts of data, they are analyzing everything about you—from the show you watched last night and the kind of coffee you purchased this morning to every Google click you made last month. Their goal is to understand you better than you understand yourself, so they can identify exactly how to shape your behavior.

Most people know *Vanity Fair* as a magazine on contemporary culture. But the title was initially penned to name a spiritual deathtrap in John Bunyan's 17th century British allegory, *Pilgrim's Progress*. In this classic work, we follow a young man named Christian as he travels from the "City of Destruction" toward the "Celestial City." His goal is to be free from the crushing burden of sin and make his way to Heaven. During his journey, Christian meets others on the path—e.g., Evangelist, Obstinate, Pliable, Help, Worldly Wiseman, Mr. Legality and his son,

Civility to name just a few—and he travels through places such as the Slough of Despond, the Hill of Difficulty and the City of Morality. If you've not read *Pilgrim's Progress*, start this week. I cannot do justice to this classic work. But I am bringing it up here for a different reason: one of the places where Christian nearly loses his way is Vanity Fair—a "city built by Beelzebub where everything to a human's tastes, delights, and lusts are sold daily." Bunyan describes Vanity Fair as a carnival-like atmosphere designed to turn unwitting people away from God. It should make us wonder. If Bunyan thought human sensibilities were being assaulted by a 17th century carnival, what would he think of the three ring circus we now call home? [6]

Fifth: We are breathing different air. The last point I'll mention is that we are absorbing different ideas and values. In some ways, this point does not belong on this list. "Breathing different air" is as much a result of items one through four as it is a stand-alone point. But in other ways it needs to be called out because things are not different simply because they are moving faster and we have more stuff, etc. Things are different because there is a new moral ecology in place. And whether you celebrate the new air or lament it, just about everyone recognizes that things are different.

Let me make my point this way: if your great grandparents miraculously showed up for dinner tonight, they would not only be shocked by smartphones, search engines, driverless cars and 24 hour news channels, they would be scandalized by the rampant consumerism and moral lethargy of our age.

In his recent best-seller, *The Road to Character, New York Times* columnist David Brooks argues that our present culture is "making it harder for us to be good." He opens by explaining that this insight came to him one night while watching an NFL linebacker do a victory dance after holding a receiver to a two-yard gain. "The defensive player did what all professional athletes do these days in moments of personal accomplishment. He did a self-puffing victory dance, as the camera lingered." This struck Brooks hard, because earlier in the day he had listened to *Command Performance*, a rebroadcast of a variety show featuring Frank Sinatra, Cary Grant, Bette Davis and others, which had been taped on the day after V-J Day (August 15, 1945). What stood out for Brooks was that even though the Allies had just completed one of the noblest military victories in human history. "… there was no chest-beating. Nobody was erecting triumphal arches."

---

6   Perhaps the more complete question is, what would he think of a culture that names one of its magazines *Vanity Fair*?

The contrast between the humility of a variety of Americans following the Allied victory with the NFL linebacker was too jarring. All he could think about as he watched the football players preening was that he was seeing more self-congratulatory behavior after a successful tackle than he had heard after the United States won World War II. He then writes:

> What was on display in *Command Performance* was more than just an aesthetic or a style. The more I looked into that period, the more I realized I was looking into a different moral country. I began to see a different view of human nature, a different attitude about what is important in life, a different formula for how to live a life of character and depth…. My general belief is that we've accidentally left this moral tradition behind. Over the last several decades, we've lost this language, this way of organizing life… We're not more selfish or venal than people in other times, but we've lost the understanding of how character is built."[7]

There are factors shaping us today besides the five I just listed,[8] but as I have already noted, my goals for this introduction are modest. I am not trying to exhaustively chronicle the moment. I am simply trying to make a case for "Going Deep." So far I've developed three points:

- We live in a new day.

- Consequently, we are being shaped by different factors.

- The result is, we are different people.

Let me now introduce two more points.

- In some ways we are less than we used to be. (Our present culture produces shallow people—think the Kardashians as opposed to Alexander Solzhenitsyn or Anne Frank.[9])

- And finally: Our present culture is increasingly pervasive and powerful.

---

7   David Brooks, *The Road to Character* (Random House, 2015), p. 7-15.

8   Among the things that might be included: 1) we now live in a global village; 2) our life expectancy has been extended; 3) families are smaller; 4) people are lonelier.

9   In one recent study, middle school girls were asked who they would most like to have dinner with. Jennifer Lopez came in first, Jesus Christ came in second, and Paris Hilton came in third. In a 2007 study, fame—which in 1976 ranked fifteenth out of sixteen as a life ambition—moved way up. Fifty-one percent of young people reported that being famous was one of their top goals. (Brooks, p. 7).

A TIME OUT TO EXPLAIN CULTURE

I've been using the term *culture* without saying much about it. Allow me to pause for a moment to make a few basic points.

- **The term *culture* describes our collective assumptions and corporate lifestyle.** Culture is how a society thinks and acts—i.e., what it values, laughs at and celebrates.

- **Culture is generally invisible to those who have grown up in it.** Until someone challenges your cultural assumptions, you are unlikely to be aware that you have any. You simply assume that everyone thinks the way you do.[10]

- **Some cultures are better than others.** Though it is politically incorrect to suggest this, some cultures are healthy and others are ill. For instance, those cultures that reward caring for the weak are better than those that advocate sacrificing infants.

- **Healthy cultures help people.** Cultures that are healthy help people live lives that work—i.e., they encourage industriousness, promote education, discourage debt, etc. Conversely, cultures that are ill promote activities that pull people down, often by promoting immediate gratification over long-term gain.

- **Our present culture is trending in the wrong direction.** As I've noted, there are lots of things about life in 21st century America that are worth celebrating. However, there are some ominous trend lines in play that we are foolish to ignore. It would be naïve to think the air we breathe is healthy and pure.[11] Our culture excels at encouraging

---

10 The joke is, if you want to know what water is like, do not ask a fish. Why? Because water is so basic to their existence—and so pervasive—that they are not even aware of it.

11 It would be easy here to cite some of the frequently sourced data points about the collapse of civilization—i.e., rise of illegitimacy, debt load, etc. But let me try to make the point without as much fanfare: The early Girl Scout handbooks preached an ethic of self-sacrifice and self-effacement. According to the handbook, the chief obstacle to happiness comes from the overeager desire to have people think about you. By 1980 the tone was quite different. That handbook was telling girls to pay more attention to themselves: "How can you get more in touch with *you*? What are *you* feeling?... Every option available to you through Senior Scouting can, in some way, help you to a better understanding of yourself... Put yourself in the 'center stage' of your thoughts to gain perspective of your own ways of feeling, thinking and acting." (James Davidson Hunter, *The Death of Character: Moral Education in an Age Without Good or Evil* (Basic Books, 2000), 103.

people to move quickly, accumulate wealth and be amused, but it does little to foster depth of character or intimacy with God.

- **Our present culture is powerful.** Just as a river current has both direction and speed, so do cultures. And in recent years, the speed has moved from Level 3 rapids to something beyond that. This means: unless you are very strong (i.e., deep!) the current will take you with it. In fact, the habits, practices and moral muscle that sustained you last year may not be enough to sustain you this one.[12]

A FEW QUESTIONS

I'm not the first person to suggest any of this. Many have done so with greater insight and clarity. And every day more people are realizing just how quickly things are changing. But because I write as the pastor of a local church, I cannot be satisfied to simply diagnose the problem, I am expected to suggest a path forward. Let me do that by posing a few questions.

How are you doing? Or to be more specific: how successfully are you navigating the rapids? There are four fairly popular approaches being embraced right now. Are you in one of these camps?

The Frenetics: The largest group out there—at least in the zip codes north of Chicago—is comprised of those who are trying to do it all: work, golf, paddle, yoga, more work, travel, volunteer, Hawks games, still more work, PTO, exercise, plant a garden, etc., etc., repeat tomorrow twice as fast. This category includes those who are making it look easy[13] and those who are flailing. (I recently asked

---

12 Allow me to illustrate this point with two stories: First, when I was young there were three TV stations and they operated during limited hours. Today children can be plugged into various media/social media outlets 24 hours a day. And the content is not the same. I watched the Dick Van Dyke Show—where Rob and Laura Petrie slept in separate beds even though they were married. Today's children are often exposed to far racier content and for far longer duration; Second, a few years back a man confided in me that he had the ability to avoid pornography when viewing it meant traveling across town to a seedy movie theater, but he did not have the moral muscle to say no when it was a click away—i.e., the habits and practices that sustained us in the past may not work in the future (or even today).

13 It is worth noting that David Brooks is convinced that many of those who appear to be successful (such as himself) are actually not so in the ways that matter most. He not only laments that he is not the person he wants to be, but reports that after teaching a class to the top graduating seniors at Princeton—students with resumes to die for (e.g., perfect S.A.T. scores, hundreds of hours of volunteer work and fluency in both Mandarin and Swahili) he discovered that they had no inner life. In fact, Brooks argues that they not only have failed to develop an inner life, they do not even have a vocabulary to talk about one.

a mom with four young boys how she was doing. I noted that Sheri and I had made the move from two boys (man-to-man defense) to three (a zone), but had no experience with four. "What is it like?" I asked. "It's like this," she said. "You are already drowning and someone throws you another baby."

The Veg-Techs: Group two is comprised of those who do not have the energy (or perhaps do not have the interest) to compete at the speed of Western culture. However, rather than cultivate a rich inner-life, they opt for entertainment. These are the folks who make it to level ninety-seven of *War Craft* and binge-watch season three of *Orange is the New Black* the first day it comes out. Of course there is nothing wrong with entertainment, just as there is nothing wrong with an occasional hot fudge sundae. But it makes a poor main course.

The Spinners: Spinners is my term for those who claim to be "Spiritual but Not Religious." (This category is also abbreviated SPNR.) People in this group tend to find modern life a bit thin but have little interest in "organized religion." I understand these inclinations, but I find the *ala carte* worldview they concoct to be thinner still.[14] Seldom does their spirituality call for much sacrifice, nor does it seem to change their political, social and economic views. Their life remains much the same, except they have supplemented it with yoga, herbal tea and whale music.

The "Leave-Me-Alones": The fourth group is made up of those who think the Amish may be on to something. They believe our common culture has become so toxic that the only sane approach is to keep the kids inside and lock the doors. As with Spinners, I am sympathetic. Raising healthy kids today does require shielding them from much of what is out there. But I am not a fan of opting out of society. I realize that there are some who think this is the best plan and that there is an historical argument to be made here.[15] But I believe Christ's call to be salt and light requires his followers to stay engaged.

Of course there are other camps (e.g. hedonists) and few are purists. Most of us

---

14 I remain confused as to how people think they can craft a coherent worldview by picking and choosing tenants of several worldviews and then acting as if their view is now true. There is no other area in which we are free to pick and choose what is true. To my way of thinking, this approach fails to even rise to the level of wishful thinking. It is simply wishing.

15 After the Vandals "stormed the gate" of the Roman Empire and civilization (as it had thus far been defined) fell, plunging Europe into what many refer to as the "Dark Ages," it was rescued by Irish monks who had to withdraw into their own enclaves. Furthermore, I admire aspects of the thinking of the "new Monastics." But I do not believe that it is time to withdraw from culture.

mix and match depending upon the day of the week. Not too surprisingly, I'd like to suggest a different option; Deep.

WHAT DOES IT MEAN TO BE DEEP?

People generally like the idea of *deep* and express a desire to become *deeper* than they are. However there is not a universally embraced definition for the term. Most agree that *deep* means more than dressing in black and attending poetry jams, and many feel drawn to the same visual images for the concept—e.g., pearl divers, tree roots and cultivated gardens. But discussions about *deep* get pretty fuzzy pretty fast. And because *deep* is not a specific biblical mandate—i.e., Jesus never said, "Be deep!"—there is no obvious place to go for a definition.[16]

When I first started thinking about deep, it was because I was drawn to the idea that if I grew deeper, my relationship with God would so profoundly shape my inner world that it would in turn shape my outer one. Instead of my environment shaping me, I would shape it; or, instead of being blown about by circumstances, I would live above them.

I no longer think this is entirely possible, nor do I even think it is ideal—after all, Jesus wept and was otherwise shaped by his circumstances. But I do think going deep points in the right direction. To get us started, I offer the following description of deep people.[17]

FIVE QUALITIES OF DEEP PEOPLE

One: Deep people are self-aware but not self-centered. Our ability to rationalize is so strong—and we can actively filter everything through such a sympathetic, ego-protecting grid—that it's quite difficult for us to see ourselves objectively. This is a problem because, while not all of our limitations would be fixed if we could see ourselves accurately, most paths forward start here. Deep people understand this and have learned how to look in the mirror without blinking.

---

16 The word *deep* shows up in many places in Scripture. Furthermore, I find the biblical idea of holiness (*kadesh*)—which initially meant weighty and implies gravitas—to be, if not a synonym, at least a complimentary term. But *deep* as I am using it is not a biblical term.

17 The great Greek philosopher Aristotle is famous for several things, one of them being his *Nicomachean Ethics*, in which he argues that often the ideal is the "golden mean"—i.e., the middle point between two extremes. I did not set out to copy his approach, but I found my description of deep leveraged his approach.

Consequently, when it comes to self-awareness, they have a clear picture of the good, the bad and the ugly. They are aware of their biases and their sins. And importantly, they have reached this point without incessant navel gazing.[18]

Two: Deep people are grounded but curious.[19] Because they are always learning, deep people are aware of new ideas, including the fads of both the marketplace and academy. But they are not easily swayed from established truth. They do not follow the crowd just because the crowd is gaining momentum. They are independent thinkers who are grounded in well-established ideas.

Three: Deep people are thoughtful yet joyful. In many circles you cannot be considered thoughtful—or deep—unless you are a pessimistic cynic. Yet God himself—who is certainly the deepest being in the entire universe—is also the most joyful. The great British writer and thinker, G.K. Chesterton understood this as well as most. Reading his work you find him both wise and childlike. Other deep people radiate a moral joy, finding contentment and hope in art, Scripture, music, nature, beauty and the success of others.

Four: Deep people are gentle yet courageous. Deep people are usually soft spoken and humble. Additionally, they tend to reject the idea that they have achieved great depth. However, this disposition should not be confused with weakness. Indeed, people of depth do not hesitate to stand up against evil, especially when they see it perpetrated upon the poor and oppressed. They may be silent when unfairly accused and dignified when others try to humiliate them, but they will not suffer those who bully others.[20] As is true with other aspects of deep people—Jesus is the prime example. He was gracious, kind, gentle and fearless at the same time.

---

18 C.S. Lewis stopped keeping a journal because he found that it made him too self-absorbed. He eventually felt that humble people "do not think less of themselves, they think of themselves less." (David Brooks makes the same point, "They [humble people] are not thinking about what impressive work they are doing. They are not thinking about themselves at all." The main point being, though deep people are self-aware, they are not self-absorbed.

19 I was tempted to write *counter-cultural* because they often are, but that often conjures up images of Haight–Ashbury and hemp man bags and that is not at all what I was thinking. When I say "counter-cultural" I mean they often find themselves moving outside the mainstream of culture.

20 In the last pages of *The Lord of the Rings* trilogy, Merry and Pippin are accompanying Frodo and Sam as they are attacked while entering the Shire. Hobbits are gentle folk, but their journey has changed them. In a way designed to show how much they have changed—deepened!—Merry and Pippin make short work of thugs they would have previously run from.

Five: Deep people are fully alive yet mindful of death. Today most people cope with their own mortality by ignoring it. Deep people do not. Instead, they not only accept their inevitable death, they leverage its punch to live more fully today.

There are other things that seem to be true of Deep People.

- They do not lead lives of conflict-free tranquility. In fact, they likely became deep in part because they suffered a great loss yet matured and grew kinder because of it.

- They are generous. Because they are aware of their own struggles and limitations, they are alert to the challenges others are facing and find ways to help them.[21]

- They do not panic. Deep people are not blown off course by a storm.

- They read a lot but do not watch much TV. They avoid the latter in part because they do not find the content uplifting, but chiefly because they are skeptical of the medium.[22]

- They have great friends. As a rule, you do not achieve great depth without great friends.

- They have some gray hair. I am not suggesting that all old people are Deep. Tragically, many are not. I am saying that it takes time to grow deep.

SO WHERE ARE YOU?

So how are you doing? Are you deep? Deepening? Do you have enough depth to successfully navigate the current of 21st century Western culture, or are you being pulled downstream pretty quickly? Are you more like the Kardashians or Alexander Solzhenitsyn? Does the thought of going deep resonate with you?

And more importantly: what are you willing to do about it? The rapids of contemporary culture are taking you to a certain spot. To end up somewhere else will require effort. Are you willing to do what is required?

---

21 My experience with Earl Massey Brown

22 Neal Postman does the best job I know of unpacking this. See *Amusing Ourselves to Death*. One of his central points is that where books (words) cultivate thought, the medium of television plays on emotions. Thus, TV itself cultivates shallowness.

QUESTIONS AND NEXT STEPS

Let me draw this to a close by trying to answer a few of the questions you may be asking. I'm also going to map out the plan. At that point you can opt in or out.

Just how religious is this going to get? I'm sure that some of you are wondering, "Why did someone give me this book in the first place? After all, I'm not religious. I don't do church. And this sounds like a "religious program?" If by religion you mean church-related or somehow intentionally linked to God, the answer is yes. As I noted earlier, I am a pastor and we will be using the Bible as the guide for what we study. Furthermore, this program is predicated on the idea that Augustine was right when he said, "Oh God, you have made us for yourself, and our hearts are restless until they find their rest in you."

However, if by religious you mean, we are doing this in order to court favor with God, then the answer is no. As a matter of fact, one of my concerns about Deep is that some people will get involved in an effort to impress God. The Bible makes it clear that we do not need to do that. In fact, we cannot. We do not reach up to God by being religious and doing good things; God reaches down to us because of His love. (I have written about this in other places and we host a series of dinner discussions about the basics of the Christian faith—with one starting later this fall. You are certainly welcome to join us for that.)[23] What I want to make clear right now is that we would not call this religious. That said, it is based on the idea that there are things we can and should do that allow us to cultivate a vital, deep relationship with God. And furthermore, this is what we all want, whether we know it or not.

But what if I'm not after that. What if I'm happy with my life right now? I don't think I want to be "deep." I believe that spiritual maturity is its own reward—that is, a deeper relationship with God leads to more joy, peace and meaning. I really believe there is a win here if you pursue it. However let me be honest and give you a pass. If you are perfectly happy right now, I'm going to have a hard time keeping your attention. Thanks for reading this far. I hope you'll stay with it. At the very least, I hope you will file this away because I'm quite certain that at some point you are going to sense a need for someone beyond yourself. But this may not be for you.

---

23 The program is called Alpha; it was started in England and has now spread around the world. Millions of people have attended this course.

So if I do take a next step, what's the plan? How much does this cost? How much time does this take? Deep is a six-week, multi-faceted program. It does not cost much, though it will take some time. As I hope is clear by now, we do not become deep people in six easy steps or over the next thirty days. What we are unfolding has three pieces to it.

Part One: This Book. In the next chapter I explain how and when to use this book. If you've looked ahead you may already know that it consists of 30 daily readings based on the Old Testament Book of Proverbs. Part one includes a daily reading from this book.

Part Two: A Discussion Group: You can read this book on your own, but you'll get more out of it if you discuss what you are reading with others. You've taken the first step in purchasing this book, or perhaps someone has given it to you. The next step is to join a discussion group—these groups begin soon and last for six weeks.

Part Three: Attend Weekly Church Services during the Series: During the same six weeks that discussion groups are meeting, the services at Christ Church will pivot around the same topics. It all links together. It is not necessary to attend church to be part of a discussion group, but it will help.

If you have more questions you can go to: christchurchil.org/deep

DISCUSSION QUESTIONS

1. What does "deep" look like? Who would you identify as "deep" and what sets them apart as such?

2. What are the five ways life has changed? Do you agree? Would you add anything to this list?

3. Of the four default approaches to life in the 21st century Western culture (The Frenetics, The Veg-Techs, The Spinners, The Leave-Me-Alones) which one do you identify with the most? If none of them, what best describes your approach to life?

4. There are five aspects of a deep person listed in the reading. Which ones are you drawn to and why? Any you disagree with? Anything you would add?

5. What might you consider adding or subtracting from your life this next week to focus on going deeper?

AN INTRODUCTION
TO PROVERBS

In a world bombarded by inane clichés, trivial catchwords, and godless sound bites, the expression of true wisdom is in short supply today. The church stands alone as the receptacle and repository of the inspired traditions that carry a mandate for a holy life from ancient sages, the greatest of whom was Solomon, and far greater than Solomon, Jesus Christ.

Bruce Waltke

DEPTH, WISDOM AND PROVERBS

Several years ago I invited Dr. Will Willimon, then the Dean of the Chapel at Duke University, to speak at a conference I was hosting for college pastors. Though Dr. Willimon studied at Yale, has written close to fifty books and was voted one of the ten best preachers in the English speaking world, he presents himself in an "ah shucks, I'm just a poor country boy" manner. "I grew up in a trailer park in Alabama. My daddy was never around 'cause he was always in jail. I don't know much," he drawls, right before he skewers you with profound insights from the passage he's preaching.

His assignment at the conference was to make it clear that no matter how hard university administrators might try to kick God off campus, he isn't leaving. Willimon made the point masterfully. He set the hook by recounting two conversations he'd been in after a recent Sunday service at Duke's chapel.

The first featured the comments a law student made to Willimon shortly after the service ended. "You convinced me," the student said. "As soon as I get back to my apartment I'm going to call my dad and tell him I'm dropping out of law school so I can work with the poor."

"Slow down friend," Willimon said. "You're doing what? You're calling who? What's gotten into you?"

The student said, "During your sermon this morning I made up my mind to drop out of law school so I can work with the poor."

"During my sermon a few minutes ago you decided to drop out of law school so you can work with the poor?" Willimon said. "And right now you are going to go call your daddy and tell him all of this?"

"Yes sir," the student replied. "I can't wait."

"And how is your daddy going to take all of this?" Willimon asked.

"Oh, he will be steaming mad, sir," the student replied. "Furious does not begin to describe it."

"Steaming. Furious. I see," Willimon said. "Young man, would you consider doing me a small favor? When you call your daddy and tell him you're dropping out of law school to work with the poor, would you leave me out of the conversation altogether?"

He then looked out over the crowd of several hundred college ministers and deadpanned, "How odd of God to use a sermon from Proverbs to change a life."

The second story was more of the same. As soon as he'd finished talking with the law student he noticed that the chapel was not completely empty. A middle-aged couple was still sitting in one of the pews. Dr. Willimon walked over and asked how they were doing, only to hear the woman say, "I'm very shaken. I just had an experience with God."

"Really," Willimon said. He then sat down and started asking questions. Before long he learned that both the husband and wife were professors; that she taught in the law school and that she was an atheist who was "only showing up to appease her husband." But to her complete surprise, during the service she had an encounter with God.

"During the service this morning at this chapel you had an encounter with God?" Willimon said.

"That's right," she replied.

"During what part of the service, specifically?" he asked. "During the singing? During the prayer?"

"During your sermon," she said.

"During *my* sermon!" he stammered. "During my sermon on Proverbs you had an encounter with God? You walked in here as an atheist lawyer. You only came to placate your husband. And during my sermon on Proverbs, God met with you."

"That's right," she said.

Willimon would later argue that neither the faculty nor the trustees could prevent God from crashing into the lives of anyone, even atheist lawyers hiding out at secular universities. But his next line was the same refrain as earlier, "How odd of God to use the book of Proverbs to change a life." He then followed that with something I suspect captured the thoughts of many of the pastors in the room. "The most remarkable thing about all of this is not that God reached out to an atheist lawyer, but that He did it through the Book of Proverbs. I don't even like the Book of Proverbs. Reading it is like getting caught on a long car ride with my mother. 'Do this! Don't do that! Save your money! Stop sleeping in!' Proverbs! How odd of God to use the book of Proverbs to change a life."

I do like the book of Proverbs; consequently I do not think it's odd that God would use it to redirect someone's life. (In fact, I think it was written for that very purpose.)[1] However, I do understand Willimon's comments. There are easier books to read—and other parts of the Bible more frequently referenced by people trying to grow closer to God—than Proverbs. I am about to ask you to set aside time every morning to read a devotion based on this collection of ancient advice. You deserve an explanation as to why.

Let me state this as simply as possible.

The goal of this series is to grow deep—that is, to strengthen our inner world in ways that lead to peace, purpose and joy.

The level of depth we are after emerges out of a vital relationship with God. We need his insight, strength and Spirit to get what we want and need most.[2]

The way forward is mysterious, but we are not left without a path. In fact, though it's challenging, the way forward is not particularly complicated. I've written about this before—and through this series I'll be setting other aspects of the path in front of you. Right now I want to focus on the part of the plan that

---

1 To quote Bruce Waltke, one of today's leading Proverbs experts and the person responsible for the quote I listed at the beginning of this chapter, "The book of Proverbs remains the model of curriculum for humanity to learn how to live under God and before humankind." Dr. Bruce K. Waltke, *The Book of Proverbs: The New International Commentary on the Old Testament* (Eerdmanns, 2004). P. xxi.

2 True depth is not just a different way of thinking, it's ultimately about becoming a different kind of person. We are unable to engineer this level of personal transformation on our own. But God can. I Thessalonians. 5:24 reads, "The one who calls you is faithful, and he will do it."

involves the book you are holding: it is based on Proverbs. I am suggesting that you read one entry every morning through the course of this series.

WHY PROVERBS?

Why are we focusing on Proverbs? Because it is filled with the kind of insights that help us go deep. Solomon (and others) reflects on what really matters and explores the insights and habits that help us cultivate the inner life we want.

THE FIRST FIVE THINGS YOU NEED TO KNOW
ABOUT THE BOOK OF PROVERBS

As I've already noted, Proverbs is an odd and frequently misunderstood book. In order to help you prepare for the daily readings that are part of this series, let me explain a few things you need to know.

One: The book of Proverbs is a collection of short, pithy statements about life. The Old Testament is comprised of three sections: The Law, the Prophets and the Writings. The book of Proverbs, along with the book of Job, the Psalms, the book of Ecclesiastes and the Song of Solomon are part of the Writings section (which is also sometimes referred to as Wisdom Literature.)[3]

Though the book contains a long introduction and ends with an acrostic poem, the largest section is a series of seemingly randomly arranged sayings that were written 3,000 years ago by King David's son, Solomon.[4]

As a young man, Solomon prayed for wisdom to be a good king.[5] God was so impressed with his request that he provided him with very unusual insight. Consequently, after Solomon became king, people came from all over the Middle East and Africa to ask him questions and to hear him speak. After his death some of his thoughts were collected into a book.[6]

---

3 These divisions are found in the Hebrew Bible. The Christian Old Testament and the Hebrew Bible are the same, but the material is arranged differently. In the Christian Bible arrangement, the Book of Proverbs is grouped with poetry.

4 Recent scholarship in the Proverbs has pointed out that the arrangement of the book is not as random as once thought, and finds various thematic connections.

5 2 Chronicles 1:6-12

6 Solomon was not the only author of the Book of Proverbs. The headings to the collections of Proverbs name several authors: Solomon, the "men of Hezekiah;" Agur and Lemuel.

Two: The Proverbs are not really proverbs. Just about every culture has proverbs, that is, short folksy statements that capture the kind of common sense insights we pass along to our children.

The Chinese say things like: *A bird does not sing because it has an answer; it sings because it has a song; or A book tightly shut is but a block of paper.*

Ben Franklin filled *Poor Richard's Almanac* with American proverbs such as: *There is no gain without pain; and Plough deep while sluggards sleep and you shall have corn to sell and to keep.*

More recently we say things like: *If you break it, you buy it; If you can't stand the heat, get out of the kitchen; and A rising tide lifts all boats.*

As odd as this sounds, the 900 pithy sayings that make up the heart of Proverbs are not actually proverbs.[7] The first way they disqualify themselves is that they are not easily understood. Indeed, some take quite a bit of work to crack. The second reason they fail is because they are poems.

I realize that the Proverbs may not strike you as poetic. But there are reasons for this. For starters, they lose some of their poetic vibe in translation. The real reason, however, is because you are expecting English poems—where the author rhymes words; these are Hebrew poems, where the author rhymes ideas.

Three: Proverbs highlight patterns and principles; they do not make promises. In spite of the fact that many people think otherwise, when Solomon writes in Proverbs 22:6, "Train up a child in the way he should go: and when he is old, he will not depart from it," he is not promising that children raised in a Christian home will remain faithful. He is observing that a child's early formation is important and often determinative. In other words, he is highlighting a pattern, not offering a guarantee. Many people do not understand this. This mistake can lead to confusion and frustration.

---

7 The title *Proverbs* is used because Jerome titled his Latin translation *Liber Proverbiorum*, and those translating his translation (The Vulgate) into English (The King James Version) followed Jerome's lead.

Note: This is not to suggest that the Proverbs are not divinely inspired. I believe they are! It's just to explain their purpose.[8] If embraced, proverbs will generally lead to a positive outcome; and if ignored you can assume you're headed for trouble.

Four: The purpose of the Book of Proverbs is to teach wisdom. In order to profit from our study—i.e. to grow in depth—we need to understand what wisdom is. And many do not. They think it is similar to information or knowledge. It is neither. Nor is it sage religious advice. Instead, wisdom is divine street smarts. Which is another way of saying, wisdom is only wisdom if it is applied. Knowing but not doing is not wisdom, it is foolishness. To paraphrase Forrest Gump: wisdom is as wisdom does.

Five: Growing wise is difficult. There are no easy steps when it comes to wisdom. And there are no money back guarantees either; quite the opposite. Many aspire, but few attain. In fact, in what is surely one of history's greatest ironies, neither Solomon's son—to whom the book is directed—nor Solomon himself!—acted wisely in the end. They may have known what to do, but they didn't do it. Mastering both the knowing and the doing is hard—not impossible, and those who turn to God will find his aid. But we need to diligently seek the insight we need; growing wise is difficult.

CLOSING COMMENTS

There are other things we could explore about Proverbs and wisdom—e.g., the proverbs are designed to be read by young men, so they have the tone of a father speaking to his son;[9] the first nine chapters of the book of Proverbs personify wisdom as a virtuous woman and then contrast her with foolishness, which is personified as a harlot; one of the major refrains of the Book is that "the fear of the Lord is the beginning of wisdom." But we will stop there, and I leave you with this thought.

---

8   The first goal of Bible study is to understand what the text means. And to do that, we must determine the genre we are working with. We are quite familiar with the various genres found in a daily newspaper—news reports, editorial, advertisements and comics. We know that when we are reading an advertisement, different rules of interpretation apply than when we are reading a news story. And the same applies to comics. Though it's common for animals to talk in cartoons, no one assumes that they can—it's just a comic. Understanding genre is an important first step in Bible study. The Proverbs are rich, divinely inspired life principles, but they are not promises.

9   I do not mean to imply that the Proverbs are only of value to young men. Not all! Only that the language has that form and feel.

We are often defined in terms of age, gender, health, occupation, IQ, net worth, etc. We would be better off to assess wisdom. Are you wise? Are you deep? Deepening? No one wants to be shallow, but the current zeitgeist does not lead into deep waters. If you want to go there, you will need to fight the current. Reading, reflecting and meditating on the divine insights found in Proverbs is a great place to start.

WEEK 1

LIVE DEEP:
FROM RÉSUMÉ VALUES
TO EULOGY VIRTUES

Total Security | Proverbs 2

All Is Not Lost | Proverbs 14

Counsel on Life and Conduct | Proverbs 22

Just In Time Providence | Proverbs 30

Read the Manual | Proverbs 8

TOTAL SECURITY

---

*My son, if you receive my words and treasure up my commandments
with you, making your ear attentive to wisdom and inclining your heart
to understanding; yes, if you call out for insight and raise your voice
for understanding, if you seek it like silver and search for it as for
hidden treasures, then you will understand the fear of the Lord and find
the knowledge of God. For the Lord gives wisdom; from his mouth come
knowledge and understanding; he stores up sound wisdom for the
upright; he is a shield to those who walk in integrity, guarding the
paths of justice and watching over the way of his saints.*

Proverbs 2:1–8 (ESV)

For as long as I can remember, I have had a constant companion that nags me in every aspect of life. This companion is not liked or invited; I just feel trapped. How should I describe my companion? Fear? Anxiety? Panic? By whatever name, the result is the same. I live with an ongoing fear in whatever what I do.

Of course I understand, most of what I sense and feel is irrational fear.

Thankfully, this passage outlines how I can tell this companion to leave me alone. My fears were human fears and were like a snare to me. In contrast to the trapped feeling stemming from my human fear, walking in the fear of the Lord brings peace. I sought to find that peace.

I began to follow the directions that are given in this passage. I learned that I had to take time in the reading and do some digging. The fear of the Lord and His knowledge do not lie on the surface, and it cannot be perceived by a superficial reading of the Bible. I started to read, study and meditate on the Scriptures. Then as understanding came, I put God's words into practice. I began to defeat my unwanted companion. I learned that the Word of God truly is living and active. I applied it to my situations, and I would see changes in my life even as I grew deeper in my relationship with God. I started to walk in and discover a new level of peace.

Every day brings new challenges and my response to them has consequences.

When I face new problems, I must decide how I will deal with them. Will I default to human approaches or trust God's wisdom and knowledge? I have learned that choosing God's way is always best even though pursuing it may seem foolish or be difficult.

As I seek God and live, I learn that much of my past fear has gone away. My fear came from ignoring the truth of God's promises and the reality of where God dwells. I cannot say that I have fully conquered fear, but my faith grows by hearing and applying Scriptures. I am quicker to discern if my circumstances are in alignment with the Word of God. Now even when I don't have an immediate answer to my circumstances, I know where it can be found. Each circumstance offers a new adventure of digging up treasures in Scripture and brings joy when I discover God's ways.

There is power in believing God's Word and standing firm on his promises until I see them manifested in the physical realm. There is peace and security in my life because I am seeing God's faithfulness and his assurance that he will work on my behalf. I press on to know him and walk in the fear of the Lord. Because he brings me total security, I can wave goodbye to my old companion. God's wisdom travels with me now.

Mette Schultz attends Christ Church Lake Forest. Mette serves the church teaching Precept Bible studies. She has been a part of the church since 2013 when she was invited to join one of the many small groups at Christ Church. She lives in Vernon Hills.

ALL IS NOT LOST

When calamity comes, the wicked are brought down,
but even in death the righteous seek refuge in God.

Proverbs 14:32

Like many people, I have faced difficult or dangerous situations and had some close calls in my life. Though none of these was close to death, I did face a difficult time of blindness when I was twenty years old. Let me explain:

In 1982, I owned a 1972 Ford Pinto station wagon (with woodgrain contact paper covering a heavily rusted body). I was living away from home for the first time and working in a summer internship. It was a beautiful day and I had parked in the driveway of the house where I rented a room from a host family. I was trying to figure out why the car wouldn't start. This was back when you could actually work on a car with a screwdriver instead of a computer.

The three primary requirements for a motor to start are "gas," "air," and "spark." I was working on spark. I found no spark at the spark plugs or the distributor and had moved over to the battery. I had filled the battery with water and I was cleaning the terminals when the battery exploded. Battery acid flew up into my eyes. I clenched them shut while burying my face in my hands, panicking, and blindly running around the yard screaming. "I have battery acid in my eyes!!!!!" My mind went totally and completely into the "ALL IS LOST" mode.

I can't be sure whether this continued for 10 seconds or 5 minutes, but no one came to my rescue. Finally my mind cleared and I thought of only one thing, "God loves me and will take care of me." This realization allowed me to do all the things that should be done in this situation. I felt my way inside the house and began flushing my eyes with water. I then called until the owner of the house came and took me to the hospital where doctors medicated and bandaged my eyes. The bandages remained on for three days. Though the doctor was hopeful, he made no predictions or promises regarding my vision.

During those three long days, I was blind. I learned to navigate the house, played with Emily, the family's one-year old daughter, and listened to TV. Listening to TV is more like reading a book since you have to provide your own pictures. I still remember my own version of "Tess of the d'Urbervilles" instead of the one that was filmed by Roman Polanski. Of course I wondered many times about whether my sight would return and what my life would be like if it didn't. The love of Jesus and the knowledge that He would always take care of me prevented the "ALL IS LOST" panic and despair from returning and overwhelming me.

God brought back my sight in full, but more importantly, he assured me that if my sight had not returned, I could still trust him.

Whenever I have that "ALL IS LOST" feeling welling up inside, I know how to quell it. This Proverb confirms that even when we are facing death, we can be sure that because of Jesus' love for us and the sacrifice he made, we can be counted as righteous and he will be our refuge. With Christ, everything changes and all is NEVER lost.

Bruce Ankenman attends Christ Church Lake Forest and has been a part of the church since 1996. He has served as both a deacon and an elder. He and his wife, Barbara, have three children who are just-in, in, and just-out of college. Both Bruce and Barbara currently serve in the middle school ministry on Sunday mornings.

COUNSEL ON LIFE
AND CONDUCT

A good name is to be more desired than great wealth, favor is better than silver and gold. The rich and the poor have a common bond, the Lord is the maker of them all. The prudent sees the evil and hides himself, but the naive go on, and are punished for it. The reward of humility and the fear of the Lord are riches, honor and life.

Proverbs 22:1-4 (NASB)

I served for seven years in hospital administration as the Director of Pharmacy at a mission hospital in Monrovia, Liberia. The hospital's reputation was so strong that I could go into virtually any local business for hospital supplies, foodstuffs, equipment, or anything else and "pay" with just my signature. All the business owners knew the debt would be paid. Though the mission station was not rich, we had a good name. This good name extended to the radio ministry and other outreach programs, including church planting and theological education.

The hospital treated Liberian government officials and business people, embassy personnel, expatriate workers, day laborers, housewives - people from across the social, religious and economic spectrum. No one was turned away. The doctor who founded the hospital, Bob Schindler ("Doctor Bob"), often would comment on our patient population, "Everyone is someone for whom Christ died." Because of this, every patient admitted to the hospital, every clinic patient, and many from the economically privileged outpatient population heard the Gospel (and many responded.) Bob was insistent that the Gospel be proclaimed, as illustrated by one of his other frequently made comments, "No matter how often we cure them, eventually they'll die."

When you're involved in medical care, you often see the consequences of good and poor choices played out in health issues. Poor healthcare choices often, in a very real sense, "punish" the naive; good healthcare choices often "protect" the prudent person from adverse medical consequences. The principle carries over into other life decisions.

Dr. Bob was a gifted surgeon who would have had a financially and professionally rewarding career in the U.S. Instead, he followed God's leading to a small, West African country to take what his U.S. peers would no doubt have called a humble position and he built a hospital that has continued to serve people and serve Christ for over 50 years. Dr. Bob and his wife, Marian, are both with the Lord, but they would say (and often did say), that their life was rich, rewarding and full. It included both of them being decorated by the Liberian government for humanitarian service. Those who knew them would also say that they unquestionably had a good name.

More than anything, I am sure it was that good name that God spoke when He said, "Well done, my good and faithful servant."

Bill Slater attends Christ Church Lake Forest and serves the church as a small group leader (co-leading with wife, Judy). He has been a part of the church since 1989. Bill and Judy live in Libertyville, with two cats, their lordships Jericho and Sasha.

JUST IN TIME PROVIDENCE

Two things I ask of you; deny them not to me before I die:
Remove far from me falsehood and lying; give me neither poverty
nor riches; feed me with the food that is needful for me, lest I be full and
deny you and say, "Who is the Lord?" or lest I be poor and
steal and profane the name of my God.

Proverbs 30:7-9 (ESV)

I had the privilege of attending college on a full-ride track and field scholarship. It was a huge benefit that afforded me an advanced education and a wonderful college experience.

But I was far away from the support of my family. Further, as an international student and scholar-athlete, I was restricted from earning personal income. It was hardly a time of excess.

After my freshman year I was able to move off-campus and save some money for personal spending. Though I didn't have much, I made sure to tithe on what I had. I was taught early on to tithe, and was experiencing God's faithful provision for all my needs.

One week in the spring of my junior year, I had just enough money either to tithe for the month or to pick up groceries for the next couple weeks—not both. I remember thinking long and hard about the many reasons why God would completely understand if I skipped the tithe just this month. Creatively I even wondered if God might accept installments. After all, I reasoned, he wouldn't want me to go hungry or be without essential provisions right?

Try as I might, I could not bring myself to avoid the commitment I had made. I just knew there was no way around it, so on Sunday, I gave as planned. At the time, a friendly couple graciously picked me up for church and drove me back to my apartment every Sunday. On that Sunday, as they dropped me off, they invited me to the back of their car, opened their trunk revealing two weeks of grocery supplies. They explained that the Lord had prompted them to purchase these because I would need them. I was simply floored. I had told no one of my predicament and decision, but God provided what I needed no sooner or later than needed. I learned a powerful lesson that day and it still serves a practical reminder of Jesus' own teaching:

> Therefore I tell you, do not be anxious about your life, what you will eat or what you will drink, nor about your body, what you will put on. Is not life more than food, and the body more than clothing? (Matthew 6:25)

That day, I learned what it meant to trust in God's providence, and wait on his timing. I also learned that God knows what we need and he blesses us (many times with more than we need) so we can honor him by extending his providence to others. This experience is a constant reminder of how God, who knows my every need, cares for me, and calls me to put him first and follow his guidance. Today, the same discipline and principle is a fundamental part of my life. God always shows up in lean times and in times of plenty, sometimes in surprisingly opportune ways, even as he is using me more and more to be a blessing to others.

William Adjei attends Christ Church Crossroads. William serves the church as a member of the worship team. He and his wife Kristy have been a part of the church since 2008 and host a small group. They have four children who range between two and eight. His family lives in Libertyville and he relishes getting in a round of disc golf any time he can.

READ THE MANUAL

Choose my instruction instead of silver, knowledge rather than choice gold, for wisdom is more precious than rubies and nothing you desire can compare with her.

Proverbs 8:10-11

In 1987 my family bought our first computer–a Leading Edge Model D. It was "loaded" with a 5¼ inch floppy drive, a monochrome monitor, and a mind-numbing 256KB of RAM. It also came with several manuals—including an entire one just for word processing.

But I treated the manual the way all 17 year old males do. Manual-schmanual.

I not only believed I was proficient because of a one hour computer class I took each week, I was confident that I was bright enough to "boldly go where no man has gone before!"

You can guess how it all ended. Within two weeks, I was back to typing my papers on a typewriter.

Let me be clear. There was nothing wrong with the computer. I simply wasn't patient enough to learn how to use it. To be more specific, I couldn't be bothered to read the manual. I pursued a quick return over a hard-earned one and got nothing.

I now read manuals for everything—DVD players, telephones, and lawn mowers. I also read the manual God wrote; the Bible.

I became a Christian a few months after my computer debacle. As soon as I found the Bible was difficult to understand, I considered giving up, but I knew this book was a life manual and contained God's wisdom to help me live more purposefully and confidently. Still, without the help of a few patient leaders and friends who modeled Bible reading, study and applying God's word to life, I would have been lost. After watching how they lived and seeing their wisdom on display, I realized the way to get what they had was to do what they did—and that meant read the Bible.

I discovered new priorities and found treasure by digging deeply into God's truth and wisdom. Though I was surrounded by other values and practices, I devoted time, quietness, watchfulness and prayer to discover the new way of wisdom the Bible offered. Though it was not as easily found, I knew when I found it that it was what my heart had been longing to find.

God's wisdom does not demand my attention, but when I read and apply the Bible, I discover a better life.

> Choose my instruction instead of silver, knowledge rather than choice gold, for wisdom is more precious than rubies and nothing you desire can compare with her. (Proverbs 8:10-11)

Before I became a Christian, my life was about getting ahead. This meant good grades, competitive college, entering a challenging career. My life was very much about the "silver," "choice gold," and "rubies" mentioned in the Proverbs passage above. Reading God's word established new priorities for me and allowed drive, goal-setting and hard work to happen only within the context of God's instruction, knowledge and wisdom. God's word is what I value most, thus it shapes every other part of my life.

Through God's wisdom, I see things differently, embrace different priorities and become more of who he wants me to be. The wisdom God offers is more valuable than gold, more precious than rubies, and well worth the time, effort and cost required to pursue it.

Jamie Morrison attends Christ Church Lake Forest. Jamie serves the church as the Pastor of Care and Connection. He has been a part of the church since 2003 when he started coming with his wife, Amy, and their four children who now range between senior in high school and 6th grade. His family lives in Lincolnshire and has a Golden Retriever named Brady.

SMALL GROUP DISCUSSION
WEEK 1 : LIVE DEEP

For the next six weeks small groups will be considering the question of what it means to be deep. In many ways the book's opening chapter addressed this, but that was Pastor Mike's perspective. The goal of what follows is not so much to debate Mike's ideas as it is to leverage them and engage those concepts. In addition to the reading, you bring to this discussion new ideas born out of the devotions, Proverbs, Bible reading, prayer and your own life experience.

Each discussion provides the opportunity to take ownership of these ideas and journey Deep.

LEANING:

What does it mean to be DEEP? Is that desirable to you?

LEARNING:

Which reading resonated most with you this week?

How would you describe the difference between résumé values and eulogy virtues?

LOVING:

What part of the sermon challenged you most or helped you grow your perspective on God's love and wisdom?

Discuss which statement is more accurate:
- God makes his people search for wisdom.
- God makes his wisdom clear and known.

LIVING:

Being as honest as you can, what are some of the deep things you do in a given week? Are you seeing changes over time?

How is wisdom found?

DIVING DEEPER:

Read Proverbs 1:1-19.

Pick four verses to share that prompt you to seek and live in the way of wisdom.

GRADUATE LEVEL:

Deep is not used in the Bible as an adjective to describe a person. What scriptural words or passages come to mind that help shape what "deep" means as we pursue it over the next six weeks?

WEEK 2

THINK DEEP:
FROM FOOLISHNESS
TO WISDOM

Wisdom Stands Out | Proverbs 1

Slow Learner | Proverbs 4

Who Will You Listen To? | Proverbs 3

Listen Closely | Proverbs 16

Preventing Heart Corrosion | Proverbs 28

WISDOM STANDS OUT

The proverbs of Solomon son of David, king of Israel: for attaining wisdom and discipline; for understanding words of insight; for acquiring a disciplined and prudent life, doing what is right and just and fair; for giving prudence to the simple, knowledge and discretion to the young—let the wise listen and add to their learning, and let the discerning get guidance—for understanding proverbs and parables, the sayings and riddles of the wise. The fear of the LORD is the beginning of knowledge, but fools despise wisdom and discipline.

Proverbs 1:1-7

Ideas and advice, the world's "wisdom," come to me in many forms each day. My regular input arrives via family and friends, but also Facebook, Instagram, television, books and magazines. I need Christian friends and a Christian counselor who help shape my life around a Biblical worldview, but more often than I'd like to admit, I neglect to seek advice from the One who knows me best.

Proverbs offers a source of God's good counsel. Proverbs 1:7 states: "The fear of the Lord is the beginning of knowledge, but fools despise wisdom and instruction." Reflecting on my mistakes (or, as I prefer to call them, my "learning experiences"), my biggest blunders occur when I fail to seek God and "despise" his wisdom and instruction. To fear him means I should respect him, obey him, submit to his discipline, and worship him.

According to research around the "rule of seven," we need to hear or see things seven times before we take action. Most marketing efforts recognize it takes consistency, effort and time to see discernible changes in consumer behavior. Though God is not "marketing" through Scripture, I find that sometimes I need a pattern of reading, reflecting and practicing God's wisdom before it becomes a regular part of my thinking and behavior. Consistency, effort and time.

Proverbs 1:2 explains the heart of Proverbs, "To teach people wisdom and discipline..." *The Message* translation titles this passage "A Manual for Living." Reading a passage once is not likely to be enough for my actions or attitudes to change. I must pray, read, listen, pray again, read again, and listen again until I hear the wisdom that God has for me. And when I hit a bump in the road, I must review again so that I can be guided to make wise choices.

I strive for peace in my life. And while my circumstances are not always so, I can experience inner peace when I feel safe: loved, protected, and forgiven by God. Alternatively, when I act foolishly, responding to situations without wisdom and instruction from my Creator, I become frustrated and anxious which results in anger, disappointment or guilt. The guilt separates me from my walk with God. If only I could consistently live as God teaches me through Solomon!

Proverbs 1:32-33 concludes:

> For the waywardness of the simple will kill them, and the complacency of fools will destroy them; but whoever listens to me will live in safety and be at ease, without fear of harm.

In the sea of input and advice, the truth and peace of these words stand out. Who wouldn't want more of that?

Beth Bolman attends Christ Church Lake Forest. She has served the church on staff, in Lighthouse, Compass and Women's Ministries. She has been a part of the church since 2005 when she was invited to attend a women's Bible study. In 2007 she started attending services with her husband Scott and four children who now range in age between 15 and 21. Her family lives in Lincolnshire and treasures family dinner.

SLOW LEARNER

*Learn to be wise, and develop good judgment. Don't forget or
turn away from my words. Don't turn your back on wisdom, for she will
protect you. Love her, and she will guard you. Getting wisdom
is the most important thing you can do! And whatever else you do, get
good judgment. If you prize wisdom, she will exalt you. Embrace
her and she will honor you. She will place a lovely wreath on
your head; she will present you with a beautiful crown.*

Proverbs 4:5-9 (NLT)

I am a slow learner. Throughout my life I have had opportunities to discover, read and enjoy God's Word, but for whatever reason, it took many years for me to truly appreciate and cherish the truth it contained.

I was exposed to God's truth in my youth through YMCA Camp where a special "Square Ceremony" highlighted four ideas, "wisdom, stature, favor with God and favor with man." Beyond that, Sunday school, sermons, confirmation classes, youth group, and Young Life meetings were also part of my introduction to God's Word and His way. But, I am a slow learner.

Getting married prompted more faith consideration and exposure to God's wisdom. However, I wasn't thinking clearly—my reflection was only a means to an end. (I told the minister a few stories about how my life had gone well thanks to God's blessings.)

Catapult another decade. After a difficult childbirth almost killed me, I claimed a new-found faith. Though I meant it and had good intentions, I did not walk my talk. (Have I mentioned the fact that I rarely, if ever, read a Bible?) I am a slow learner.

I cruised through more years of attending church and felt held by the loving arms of God, but made no effort to gain wisdom from reading God's Word.

Finally, the rubber met the road. Some major health and family issues squeezed me into a place where I suddenly needed God. (Yes, I realize I needed Him all along, but through this the fact that I really needed him finally became apparent to me.)

I was growing in my faith, but because of my husband's career we moved our family far away from all the resources I'd developed for spiritual growth over 25 years.

At this crossroads I made the decision to try Christ Church. It was there I heard a simple suggestion: "read the Bible and pray, each for 10 minutes a day." I won't say I have always adhered to this basic plan, but I am wise enough to try.

I have been deliberate about praying more. As I drive I use thematic sights to remind me to pray for certain people. I also signed up for the "Our Prayer" ministry with Guideposts which helps me grow in prayer.

To help keep my commitment, I found a unique way to supplement my Bible reading. I bought a recording of the New Testament read by actors in an expressive, engaging manner.

Proverbs 4:5-9 recommends that if I choose to embrace God's Word, I can develop good judgment, have protection, be exalted and honored, and be decorated with a wreath or crown upon my head. In other words, I will be safer from the world's terrors, make better decisions, feel lifted up and bear the marks of a wise woman. (And I don't just mean wrinkles and gray hair.)

As I grow, people can actually trust me to give them wise counsel based in wisdom and backed up by my experiences and Scripture.

It may have taken half a century for me to figure out how to walk my talk, but that's okay—I've always been a slow learner.

Jen Richards attends the :01 service. Jen serves in the Women's Ministry and has been a partner with our missions work in India. She has been a part of the church since 2011. Jen and her husband Randy have been married for 30 years and live in Lake Bluff. They have three adult children. They also have a family dog, who has his own blog titled, PAWS: Moments with Magnus Pym.

WHO WILL YOU LISTEN TO?

The fear of the LORD is the beginning of wisdom, and knowledge of the Holy One is understanding. For through me your days will be many and years will be added to your life. If you are wise, your wisdom will reward you; if you are a mocker, you alone will suffer.

Proverbs 9:10-12

Some years back, I attended a neighborhood Bible study on wisdom. The study focused on Proverbs 31 and "the woman of noble character." In it we read a chapter in Proverbs each day. When reading Proverbs 9 something struck me. At the highest point of the city, wisdom and folly BOTH call out to the simple.

Though the invitation from wisdom and folly is the same ("Let all who are simple come and dine with me and you will be rewarded"), the outcomes are vastly different. Wisdom's reward is "life," "understanding," "wisdom," and "knowledge." Folly's reward is the opposite—"suffering," "death," and the "grave."

Proverbs 9:10 tells us that the fear of the LORD is the beginning of wisdom. That fear is a reverent obedience to him; an awe and attraction to him. Folly, by contrast, is a lack of good sense or judgement. The Bible tells us that folly is undisciplined and lacks knowledge. Yet continually both voices call out to us.

In all my roles as wife, mother, friend, Christian, and servant, I'm faced with these two choices. Will I listen to God's way or the world's way? How will I choose?

There are several habits that help me hear God's voice. When reading my Bible I learn about God and his character. This reminds me of his promises; it gives me strength and courage to choose wisely. When I spend time praying, reflecting, reading a devotion, journaling or listening to music about God, I gain understanding and knowledge about him. Going to church to worship with other believers, being in a small group, attending a Bible study, and choosing friends who hold me accountable to God's standards all center me and help me grow deeper.

I know I can still choose foolishly—too much social media, television, shopping on the web, or pouring myself into things that have no eternal value. Folly entices me to choose this and act selfishly, spend frivolously, envy others, go for instant gratification and ignore the consequences.

When I choose wisdom, the One who put his Spirit in my heart gives me love, joy, peace, patience, kindness, goodness, faithfulness, gentleness and self-control. These help me be a good wife and teammate to my husband. They help me love sacrificially and give me confidence. They allow me to speak the truth into my kids, pray for them and warn them about the consequences of folly. Wisdom allows me to be sensitive to others who are struggling as I have struggled. Knowledge makes me teachable enough to receive godly advice from others.

There are two voices competing for our attention. We are free to choose. Choose wisely.

Mistele Bloom attends Christ Church Crossroads. She serves the church in the meal train ministry, boiler room prayer time, participates in a small group, and substitutes in the summer in the children's program. She has been a part of the church since 2004 (with a four year absence due to her husband's career in the Navy) and attends with her husband John and four kids who range from age 14-20. Her family lives in Libertyville with their Goldendoodle, Libby.

LISTEN CLOSELY

The hearts of the wise make their mouths prudent, and
their lips promote instruction. Gracious words are a honeycomb,
sweet to the soul and healing to the bones. There is a way
that appears to be right, but in the end it leads to death.

Proverbs 16:23-25

"Have you ever thought about going to seminary?"

Until I was asked that question about five years ago, the answer had been no. I found myself dealing with shock and disappointment after not getting a job I was seeking. The career path I thought I was taking was now shut before me, and the plan I had for my life was not working out as I intended. I was having breakfast with my friend and searching for answers about what went wrong. It was his advice that opened up a new door in my life that I had never even considered. Listening to his counsel brought me where I am today. The words of my wise friend were a refreshing breath for my soul used by God to move me in a new direction.

When Solomon asked for and was granted wisdom, word spread quickly around the world that he had insight and understanding which far surpassed anyone else who lived. As a result, people started turning to him for advice. 1 Kings 4:34 says "From all nations people came to listen to Solomon's wisdom, sent by all the kings of the world, who had heard of his wisdom." That's the thing about wise people, their words are worth hearing.

Solomon is clear that the way of wisdom is "sweet to the soul." But he also warns there is a way that "appears" right but is dangerous. Life is full of choices. These verses warn us to listen closely to those with wisdom, as their words will help move us in the right direction, not just the one that appears to be right.

I was intentional about inviting my wise friend to breakfast. He had given me wise advice for years. In fact, to this day I would count him as one of the wisest and most discerning people I know. He is the man I turn to when I need to talk through a decision. Over the years he had helped me seek out the direction I should be going. More recently, my wife Kellie and I reached out to him while going through the adoption process of our daughter, Leah. He was instrumental during my decision to accept the role of Campus Pastor here at Christ Church Highland Park. A wise friend is a valuable friend indeed.

I cannot imagine my life without someone to turn to for counsel. If there is no one you can turn to, now is the time to start looking. It may take some time to see the wisdom of others, but eventually you will come to know that you can trust their word. Once you have that person in your life, my advice is simple: listen to them closely.

Dan Syvertsen attends Christ Church Highland Park. Dan serves the church as the Campus Pastor. He has been a part of the church since 2012 when he started coming with his wife Kellie. He and Kellie have just adopted their first child, Leah. His family lives in Highland Park and have a dog named Shea, named after the old stadium of the New York Mets.

PREVENTING HEART CORROSION

He who conceals his sins does not prosper, but whoever confesses and renounces them finds mercy. Blessed is the man who always fears the Lord, but he who hardens his heart falls into trouble.

Proverbs 28:13-14

As an aircraft mechanic for over 20 years, I've had significant experience "troubleshooting"—systematically tracking down problems in components or systems. Much of aircraft maintenance is designed to prevent problems, but every so often there will be a click or clatter, a shake or shimmy, a pulling or pushing that a pilot will tell us about after a flight. This is simply the aircraft saying, "Hey, I have a problem, could you fix this?"

But the more insidious problems are the ones without symptoms—the ones you can't see or feel or hear in flight. The aircraft silently keeps doing its job, all the while masking a deficiency. Corrosion is one such problem. It can start on the inside of the metal frame, weakening structural integrity until something cracks or breaks. Aircraft maintenance organizations know it is wise to spend time and money on detailed inspections with expensive equipment to find these corrosion issues before there is a costly catastrophe.

So it goes in our dealings with sin.

Are we willing to admit our sins and ask God for help? He offers cleansing, forgiveness and restoration. Or do we conceal the issues—justifying, denying, blaming, ignoring, and deceiving ourselves and others?

When we hide, we expose our hopelessly misguided theology. God always knows, and He doesn't let dirt pile up under the carpet for long. We dishonor Him when we fabricate our cover stories and alibis. There is simply no blessing in this, only pain. The more we hide, the better we become at lying, the harder the heart becomes and the deeper we delve into that which would destroy us. The conscience is soon too weak to make any difference in our thought and behavior. Hiding our sin multiplies problems upon problems until one day everything breaks and we go down in flames.

The best thing we can do is stop hiding and confess our sins, first to God and then to a brother or sister in the Lord whom we can trust. Be vulnerable with someone as soon as you realize you have blown it. No doubt it is harder after living a secret life for many years, but if your heart has experienced a moment of softness and conviction, don't let that moment get away. Act now, before corrosion runs its full course and the wing falls off the plane. God is completely aware of the situation and can handle all the damage and difficulty of bringing your sins into the light.

But confession is only half the battle. The one who fears the Lord, according to these verses, also renounces his sins. To live under the grace of God in Jesus Christ certainly means that our sins are forgiven. This is what puts the good in the Good News. But this amazing grace does not give us license for further sin. Sin is not to be our master (Romans 6:14). An airplane with corrosion issues cannot be put back into service just by finding the corrosion; the corrosion must be removed and new metal structure patched in its place. In the same way, the woman who confesses her sin cannot possibly be restored to good spiritual health if she is not also determined root it out and follow righteousness.

It is time to be restored. It is time to fear the Lord, confess, renounce sin, and find mercy.

Jim Levander attends Christ Church Crossroads. Jim serves the church as an AWANA leader and is working through Trinity's MDiv program. He has been a part of the church since 2013 when he started coming with his wife (Becky) and two boys who are in 5th & 6th grade. His family lives in Lindenhurst and he likes cycling the trails and playing disc golf.

SMALL GROUP DISCUSSION
WEEK 2 : THINK DEEP

Wisdom sits at the foundation of being a person of depth. Unlike the images of a wise hermit dispensing counsel from a desert mountain, we are looking to discover a wisdom that interacts and integrates with our day to day life. Where can that wisdom be found?

LEANING:

Whose wisdom (a person's, not God's) has helped you navigate life well? How was that wisdom shared with you?

LEARNING:

Which proverb or devotion did you most connect with or feel inspired by this week? What did you like? What did you learn?

How would you differentiate wisdom and knowledge? Is one better? Why or why not?

LOVING:

What part of the sermon challenged you most or helped grow your perspective on God's love and wisdom?

Read Job 28:1-28. How would you describe the wisdom of this chapter? Can you summarize the most important points being communicated?

LIVING:

Let's assume wisdom might allow you to understand and solve a challenge you are facing. For which situation in your life would you like more wisdom?

How do wise people become wise? How could you find wisdom to help with the challenge you identified above? (Consider James 1:5)

DIGGING DEEPER:

Read 1 Kings 3 and 1 Kings 4:29-34. What was God's offer to Solomon? Would you choose as he did? What was the result of Solomon's decision?

GRADUATE LEVEL:

Review Ecclesiastes 7:1-8:1 and Ecclesiastes 12:9-14. What sparks the writer's (likely Solomon's) love of wisdom? What are the central themes you see?

WEEK 3

WORK DEEP:
FROM SLOTH
TO DISCIPLINE

PROVIDING FOR YOUR FUTURE

Go to the ant, you sluggard; consider its ways and be wise!
It has no commander, no overseer or ruler, yet it stores its provisions
in summer and gathers its food at harvest. How long will you lie there,
you sluggard? When will you get up from your sleep? A little sleep, a
little slumber, a little folding of the hands to rest—and poverty will
come on you like a thief and scarcity like an armed man.

Proverbs 6:6-11

Do you remember 1986? 1999? 2006?

In those years, everyone wanted to be the next big investment banker, internet mogul or real estate investor. There was no other way to go but up. To quote Alan Greenspan, an "irrational exuberance" filled the air. Opportunities were every-where, and everyone was *one deal away* from making it big.

Then came 1987, 2000 and 2007.

I remember walking to class at my graduate business school the morning of October 19, 1987. Outside of the building, someone had hung a bed sheet with the words spray painted "Don't Panic." When I walked into the building, no one was in class. They were all huddled around the televisions watching the largest percentage decline ever in the Dow Jones Industrial Index. Half of my savings for graduate school was wiped out that day.

But God's Word has practical advice and application even for times like this.

Solomon teaches us an important lesson in Proverbs 6. To make his point, he uses the least of all creatures, the ant, to illustrate God's wisdom. By God's design, the ant naturally stores food ahead, saves and provides for the future, without any leaders commanding them. We see in nature and in history that there are periods of growth and decline, feast and famine. God instructs us to be prepared for this cycle, to save in times of prosperity to help us through times of recession. This is a simple message in theory, but difficult to apply in practice. In times of prosperity, many people choose to "go all in." They pursue unbelievable deals that sound too good to be true. Yet in times of recession, you may hear of the hardships as those same people are losing their homes or, worse, their life savings.

In Proverbs 6:6-11, we hear God's instructions for saving in prosperous times and living well through recessions. Diligently and consistently save in prosperous times, no matter how small the amount. These savings will help you survive through the lean times that will inevitably follow. This strategy may not sound exciting, but it is proven to work. Proverbs 21:5 says "Steady plodding brings prosperity. Hasty speculation brings poverty." In Genesis 41, Joseph advises Pharaoh to save in seven prosperous years to survive seven years of famine. By steadily saving and investing responsibly, our savings can grow and support us in years when we need it.

Andrew Dun attends Christ Church Lake Forest. Andrew serves the church as a member of the Deacon Board, Church Treasurer and Financial Peace Coordinator. He has been a part of the church since 2002 when he started coming with his wife, Carolyn, and 2 children who are now 21 and 23 years old. His family lives in Lincolnshire.

FACING MY REAL REALITY

The proverbs of Solomon. A wise son makes a glad father, but a foolish son is a sorrow to his mother. Treasures gained by wickedness do not profit, but righteousness delivers from death. The Lord does not let the righteous go hungry, but he thwarts the craving of the wicked. A slack hand causes poverty, but the hand of the diligent makes rich. He who gathers in summer is a prudent son, but he who sleeps in harvest is a son who brings shame. Blessings are on the head of the righteous, but the mouth of the wicked conceals violence.

Proverbs 10:1-6

When reflecting on the discipline of living out biblical wisdom, I have found it helpful to think along these lines: biblical wisdom calls us to face our "real reality" and deal with it head on according to the Lord's direction and truth.

To explore what I mean by "real reality," let's think of two big aspects of the overarching narrative of the Bible.

The first aspect is that God has *revealed* himself to us—fallen and sinful as we are. That's good news. God has not left us alone with the devastating consequences of our sin, which would separate us from him eternally. No, God has revealed himself and his way to us, that we might effectively deal with our problem of sin and renew our relationship with him. This is heady; it is full of eternal hope. Through faith in Jesus Christ, and by his grace, we have an actual, palpable hope of eternal life in heaven with God.

This means that whatever the nature of our present life, if we belong to Christ, our current life is not the end of the story. In a sense, it's only the beginning of our eternal story with God.

In the meantime, if we have professed faith in Christ and live with this eternal hope of heaven, God still calls us to live out our Christian calling here on earth, in this life we have before us.

That brings us to a second major aspect of the Bible's story: that in revealing to us a way of eternal salvation, God has also made it possible for us to live *transformed* lives in the present. The Bible contains practical texts that call us to think about (and act upon) what our life should look like in such day-to-day spheres as family, work, and relationships. This is where I see biblical wisdom playing a major role.

As a follower of Christ, for instance, I am certainly firm in my hope for heaven, based on the grace of Christ and his work on the cross. At the same time, Jesus still calls me to grow in godliness in this life. This is when the idea of grasping my "real reality" starts to play a role.

Often, if I am honest, I find that I am quite good at constructing alternative realities for myself—precisely because I don't want to face a particular "real reality," which usually involves some form of sin.

If I am dealing with a particular sin issue, it is certainly easier to try and ignore it, to try and rationalize it away, or just artificially downplay its severity to my soul. That's creating an artificial reality.

Biblical wisdom comes to us and helps us shatter those false realities and enables us to get at the "real reality" that we need to confront.

Take my life as a father: it might be easier for me to ignore or quickly pass over the mistakes my children make or the sinful options they might choose in life. But biblical wisdom reminds us that walking with God in this life also entails practically leading our children in coming face-to-face with their "real reality" and helping them actually deal with it.

The first six verses of chapter 10 introduce the full collection of short wisdom sayings in the book of Proverbs (the first nine chapters serve as the introduction to the whole book). If you read these six verses and meditate on them, you will quickly see that "false reality" and "real reality" can stand as underlying and contrasting themes.

For instance, in the particular case of Proverbs 10:1, we could state that wisdom is a source of *joy* for a parent because a child has dealt with his or her "real reality" and has grown in godliness from it. In contrast, this verse also reminds us that folly (the opposite of biblical wisdom) is a source of *sorrow* for a parent, when a child has not effectively dealt with a sinful, false reality. Implicit here is that both parents and children are actively engaged in seeking to live out godly wisdom on a daily basis.

May the Lord guide us all as we develop our ability to honestly face the illusions of a sinful reality and break through, with daily discipline, to the "real reality" of walking in his way of wisdom!

Nathan Clayton attends Christ Church Lake Forest. Nathan serves the church as a small group leader and as an active member of the worship and arts ministry team. He has been a part of the church since 2003 when he started coming with his wife Maureen and their 4 children, who now range in age from a sophomore in high school to a 4th grader. His family lives in Lake Forest and they have a Bernese Mountain Dog named Phoebe and a King Charles Cavalier Spaniel named Samson.

SO MUCH TIME, SO LITTLE TO DO

From the fruit of their lips people enjoy good things, but the unfaithful have an appetite for violence. Those who guard their lips preserve their lives, but those who speak harshly will come to ruin. A sluggard's appetite is never filled, but the desires of the diligent are fully satisfied.

Proverbs 13:2-4

When I was a freshman in college, I noticed a curious pattern emerging in my life. As each new semester would draw to a close, I would set goals that I wanted to accomplish over the upcoming break. I would pick a few books to read, identify a few projects to work on, and resolve to spend more time reading my Bible and praying.

After a semester packed full of classes, sports, clubs, and church, the slower pace of life back home should have allowed me to accomplish my modest goals. And yet at the end of each break, I found myself woefully unsatisfied with my progress. In fact, when it came to my devotional time, I almost always gave less time each week to prayer and Bible reading while I was on break than I did during the school year.

At first, I couldn't understand why I was able to accomplish so much less when I had so much more time. Then I finally realized it: the demands of college forced me to exercise discipline in certain areas of life, and that discipline flowed over into other areas as well. But when I entered a break and the need for discipline lessened, I was unable to be disciplined in the areas that mattered.

In Proverbs 13:2-4, we find the wisdom that I lacked as a freshman in college: fulfilling our desires requires discipline. When discipline slips, we find ourselves consistently falling short of our goals.

But this passage does far more for us than highlight the consequences of poor time management. It also gives us insight into how we manage our character development. Specifically, we see that those who lack the ability to regulate their words are headed for destruction as quickly as those who are unable to regulate their time.

It is no accident that the writer of Proverbs chooses to focus on the importance of our words. Our words have great power. As James says, the tongue is like the rudder on a large ship—though it is small, it is able to steer the ship wherever the captain chooses. If we wish to be deep people—men and women of great character—we must start by disciplining our tongues. That discipline will then flow over into the rest of our character, and from there to the rest of our lives.

For many us of, becoming a person who "guards his or her lips" may fall fairly low on our priority list. If that sounds like you, spend some time thinking about verse 3, "Those who guard their lips preserve their life, but those who speak rashly will come to ruin." If we don't learn to control our tongue, it will control us, and we won't like where it leads us. The road to becoming a person of great character starts with being disciplined in our words. Don't neglect this essential part of the process.

Dan Westman attends Christ Church Lake Forest. Dan serves the church as a leader at SHYG and The :01. He has been a part of the church since 2011 when he started coming with his wife Linzy. Dan and Linzy live in Vernon Hills, and he loves playing tennis, golf, and Settlers of Catan.

TRAINING

Better to meet a bear robbed of her cubs than a fool bent on folly. Evil will never leave the house of one who pays back evil for good. Starting a quarrel is like breaching a dam; so drop the matter before a dispute breaks out. Acquitting the guilty and condemning the innocent— the Lord detests them both. Why should fools have money in hand to buy wisdom, when they are not able to understand it?

Proverbs 17:12-16

My family and I recently had the incredible experience of riding "The Cog" to the top of Pike's Peak in Colorado. This hour-and-fifteen-minute train ride winds up the side of the mountain. The incline is so steep at points that we were pressed into our seats. The ascent includes beautiful waterfalls, amazing rock formations, clear mountain lakes, and drop-offs that literally took our breath away. The beauty is so captivating we hardly noticed the dropping temperature. As we passed the tree line the conductor informed us of an upcoming marathon that runs up and down the mountain.

I am serious about fitness and wondered how I'd do in such a race. However, once we got to the top and I began chasing my daughter around, my hopes faded almost as quickly as my breath. Though the views were of course breathtaking, I was surprised at the literal "breathtaking" feeling brought on by the altitude. I wasn't overexerting myself, but with the low oxygen levels I felt winded. I thought of the marathon again and wondered, "How does anyone do that length at this altitude?"

I know the answer. A person doesn't run this because they think they are physically fit or because they plan to try really hard. The only way to run a marathon, especially one up Pike's Peak, is to enter into a time of training. The skills, experience and endurance necessary would only come by deliberate effort.

As I processed this during our descent, I began to think about how often we try to run the marathon of life unprepared or untrained. Being unprepared manifests itself in many different ways. I think one of the most common ways we are untrained in western culture is that we *think* we *are* trained.

We train for climbing the corporate ladder or having a certain amount of money in savings or living in a certain area or just simply trying to fit in. We set these things as our goal and we go. In doing so we miss the one true training to which we are called. As followers of Jesus, we are to train. We do this by knowing our God and pursuing his Kingdom. A big key to this pursuit is the Bible. If we are not training to be spiritually fit, then everything we do is simply foolish. No matter what we are basing our marathon of life training on—if it's not Jesus, it is foolishness. To continue to base your training on anything but Jesus is to be a fool.

It's interesting what the Bible says about fools. Proverbs 17:12 states that it is "better to meet a bear robbed of her cubs than a fool bent on folly." We live in a culture where so many around us are training for a life of no lasting importance. But to tell them otherwise would mean getting made fun of or even being viewed as an outcast. This is a modern day civilized fool bent on folly. Better to meet a bear separated from her cubs than a fool so bent on pursuing emptiness because a fool may actually convince you his way is right.

Jon Kimmel attends Christ Church Lake Forest. Jon serves the church as the Middle School Pastor. He has been a part of the church since 2013 when he started coming with his wife Megan and two year old daughter Baelyn. His family lives in Mundelein and they love to be outside and active.

HARVEST TIME

It is to one's honor to avoid strife, but every fool is quick to quarrel.
Sluggards do not plow in season; so at harvest time they look
but find nothing. The purposes of a person's heart are deep waters,
but one who has insight draws them out.

Proverbs 20:3-5

This summer my crew piled into the van for two weeks of summer vacation in Florida. For a few days around the July 4th holiday, three generations of family gathered together. We ate a lot of food, made a lot of noise, and got a lot of sand in the van. We also spent a lot of evenings staying up way too late catching up, telling stories, and watching old family videos.

I love when we're able to get everyone together. It doesn't happen often enough, but when it does it's a real celebration. We celebrate birthdays, new additions to the family, victories at home, school or work—whatever good things are going on in each other's lives. And we have a great time doing it.

As I reflect on the Proverbs above in the context of my extended family, it occurs to me that what we're really celebrating are decades of hard work and generally wise choices, at least when it comes to the big things in life.

It is to one's honor to avoid strife, but every fool is quick to quarrel. (Proverbs 20:3)

More often than not, my parents and grandparents have chosen to avoid strife rather than quarrel, even though there have been countless opportunities to battle over one issue or another. Just thinking about things I've said and done, it amazes me how much grace I've received and how many undeserved opportunities I've enjoyed. I hope and pray that I will display the same kindness and self-control in my parenting (and eventually grand-parenting if we make it that far!).

Sluggards do not plow in season; so at harvest time they look but find nothing. (Proverbs 20:4)

Right now is a harvest time for my parents, but it didn't come quickly or without cost. When my siblings and I were growing up, my parents made a priority of being present in our home and keeping us involved in church. And they didn't bend in these commitments. It meant career sacrifice as my dad turned down promotions in order to be home every night. It meant scheduling other activities around church whether it was popular with us kids or not. It meant consistently establishing a rhythm of life that trained all of us to value our faith and family above everything else. To me, they set a great example of plowing in season in order to reap a rich harvest of joy in our family today.

Obviously not everyone's family story is like mine. For any number of reasons, you may not be experiencing a season of harvest. Or you may have little faith that the work you're now doing will yield fruit in the future.

Whatever the case, remember it is the sluggard who finds nothing at harvest, not the diligent worker. So we should all put our hand to the plow, knowing the work we do today will not be fruitless, and it's never too late to begin. As the Apostle Paul says, "Let us not become weary in doing good, for at the proper time we will reap a harvest if we do not give up" (Galatians 6:9).

Anson Hanbury serves the church as Adult Life Pastor. He has been a part of the church since 2014 when the merger with Crossroads took place and he started coming with his wife, Dina, and five children who range between 11 years old and 8 months. His family lives in Libertyville and Anson and Dina love to ballroom dance.

SMALL GROUP DISCUSSION
WEEK 3 : WORK DEEP

One of the first questions asked when people are meeting is, "What do you do?" While this helps people learn something about each other, it has the unwanted byproduct of narrowing our perspective of work around paid employment. The deep person works, but how they work and what they do through that work should say more about them than simply answering, "what are you paid to do?"

LEANING:

What is something that may feel like "work" to some people but is something you do easily, joyfully or well?

LEARNING:

Which Proverb or devotion did you most connect with or feel inspired by this week? What did you like? What did you learn?

What does "work" mean when associated with God in a context like Ephesians 2:8-9? What does "work" mean in the following verse, Ephesians 2:10? What challenges may be associated with this word "work?"

LOVING:

What part of the sermon challenged you most or helped grow your perspective on God's love and wisdom?

Why are Paul's words in Colossians 3:23-24 helpful to shape our life?

LIVING:

Take some time to narrow down and describe your top 4 life goals. To what extent are these important goals the first priority each week, month, year, etc.?

Are they S.M.A.R.T. goals? (search S.M.A.R.T. goals on the web if the concept is unfamiliar to you)? Is there a way to know if you are progressing towards or meeting your goals?

DIGGING DEEPER:

Colossians 1:9-12 provides a glimpse of Paul's prayer for the Colossians. To what extent does this reflect what Christ may also desire from us? If these prayers were answered for you, would you feel satisfied with life?

GRADUATE LEVEL:

What is the difference between training and trying? Read 1 Corinthians 9:24-27. Paul references training in his metaphor. What does this mean spiritually?

WEEK 4

DEEP INSIGHT:
FROM TEMPORAL
TO ETERNAL

Grumbling and Grace | Proverbs 3

A Prayerful Journey | Proverbs 18

Pursuing God | Proverbs 19

Balance | Proverbs 24

Wise Guy | Proverbs 25

GRUMBLING AND GRACE

Let love and faithfulness never leave you; bind them around your neck, write them on the tablet of your heart. Then you will win favor and a good name in the sight of God and man. Trust in the Lord with all your heart and lean not on your own understanding; in all your ways acknowledge him, and he will make your paths straight.

Proverbs 3:3-6

Years ago in North Carolina, I co-led a college ministry with a woman named Brenda who asked me to put together a monthly newsletter and send it to the students. After the newsletter had been distributed, she called with several suggestions, corrections, edits and rewrites. I was livid. "How dare you! I did exactly what you asked me to do. You asked me to write it and send it out and I did—who are you to come in after the fact with this criticism? If you wanted control, you should have done it yourself." The words were spoken in a harsh and elevated tone, with an angry backdrop and through tears. I was angry, my pride and ego were bruised, and I was ready to walk away from ministering with her.

I expected her to respond in a like manner. Rather, she listened to my outburst, apologized, and hung up the phone. Several minutes later, she called back. Great, I thought—now I would receive the satisfaction of having a screaming match with her. Wrong. Her tone was gentle as she spoke. "Mary, I have thought about what you said and you are right. You did exactly what was asked and you did a great job. The students will be blessed. My perfectionism kicked in and the edits that I suggested are not only unnecessary but would make the newsletter too corporate. Thank you for your hard work. I hope you can forgive me. I love you."

What just happened? How could this woman extend love and grace to me at a point where my selfish pride had kicked in and taken over my mouth and motive? Her response overwhelmed me and opened my eyes to grace; I had not experienced anything like this before. She had learned something in her Christian walk that I had yet to learn: to lean into the character of Christ—as contrary as it was to the world—and to display his character regardless of the attack she faced. Her actions planted in me a desire for that same characteristic of displaying love and modeling humility in tough situations.

Since then there have been many situations when God has asked me to show grace where human wisdom would not agree. Because of Brenda's response to me, I understand grace differently.

God's ways are not our ways. Let us lean into him for understanding; let us trust that he will direct our path and show us how to model his teachings through himself, his Word, and other people.

Mary Hamrick attends the Lake Forest campus of Christ Church. Mary serves on the church staff as the Director of Connections. She has been a part of the church since 2010. Mary has four adult children and eight grandchildren. She lives in Vernon Hills and enjoys speaking nationally at women's conferences on living a life of obedience in today's chaotic world.

A PRAYERFUL JOURNEY

*The name of the Lord is a fortified tower; the righteous
run to it and are safe. The wealth of the rich is their fortified city;
they imagine it a wall too high to scale. Before a downfall
the heart is haughty, but humility comes before honor.
To answer before listening—that is folly and shame.*

Proverbs 18:10-13

In 2010 I was asked to be on a prayer team with a group of people I considered to be "prayer warriors." I was convinced that their faith was not something I could comprehend or even possibly achieve. I was overcome with shame and fear just thinking about praying in front of them. What would I say? What would they think of me if I used the wrong words? Would they lay hands on me? How much time was this going to take out of my day? I knew some key Scriptures in the Bible, but prayer was not something I knew how to do.

I agreed to join the team knowing it was the right thing to do. As the word "yes" flowed from my mouth, my first thoughts went directly to figuring out how I could minimize my commitment. For the first three months, I maintained that my children and my to-do list remained the priority so I could excuse myself from meetings. Then I was asked to continue on the prayer team indefinitely. My patience was being challenged. I began to negotiate with God. I bargained with him that if he answered my prayer in that moment, I would stay on the team. If not, I was all done. In God's glory, he answered my prayer almost immediately. I can still recall feelings of the tears, shock and awe in that moment. He kept his part of the bargain so I kept mine. I stayed on the team.

Over the next few months, God's mystery of prayer was revealed to me through each one of the prayer team members. We discussed types of prayer and application, we prayed through Scripture, they shared prayer life experiences, and we prayed for one another, our church, our community and the world. It was during this period of time that I discerned a distinct shift within me. Through prayer I deepened my relationship with the Lord. I was listening and growing to know him more. I felt God was working on my heart through his Holy Spirit. He was equipping me with his wisdom and I was experiencing grace. As the shame and fear dissipated, I wasn't trying to make prayer fit into my day anymore. It had simply become part of my life. Now I pray whenever or wherever the Spirit prompts me.

As I reflect back, I am thankful that God gave me this prayer journey with this team. I continue to be honored by his provision and unconditional love even as I willfully negotiated against what he knew was best for me. Now I desire to be a prayer warrior. I am humbled that God's vision of his Kingdom here on earth and his character can be transformational in each of us. We must stop imagining the walls are too high to scale, have faith and let him show what he can do.

The name of the Lord is my strong tower.

Lachele Kawala attends Christ Church Lake Forest. She serves where prayer is needed. She has been a part of the church since 2002. Lachele is married to David and has three children, who range from age 10-24. Her family lives in Lake Bluff and has a Portuguese Water Dog named Jax.

PURSUING GOD

*Listen to advice and accept discipline, and at the end
you will be counted among the wise. Many are the plans
in a person's heart, but it is the Lord's purpose that prevails.*

Proverbs 19:20-21

When I read these two verses, two thoughts come to mind: my propensity to make lists and plans and the many times my plans have not worked out the way I thought they would.

I love using time management and planning tools. Remember the Day Planner, Franklin Planner, Day Runner and Day Timer? I used each one at some point, although currently I use digital tools on my phone and iPad. I especially enjoy using tools to make to-do lists for each day, week and month. In fact, if I finish something that is not on my list, I add it and cross it off, just for the fun of it! When I have a plan, I feel like I am in control of my life.

However, we all know that many of our plans don't turn out the way we want them to. Three years ago, my family shared a delicious Easter brunch with my parents. My father had recently turned 80, and he felt the need to explain why he wasn't eating as much as usual. He said he planned to live an active, healthy life, so he was on a calorie restricted diet and was taking several vitamins and supplements based on longevity articles he had been reading. A month later, he fell, hit his head and had a brain bleed due to blood thinners. It was a lengthy recovery process, and he is now in an assisted living facility. Clearly, the fall was not part of my father's plans.

So, how should we make plans? These verses provide a straightforward approach. First, we must listen to wise counsel or good advice and then receive it. Where do you find good advice? Proverbs 1:7 gives us an answer: "The fear of the Lord is the beginning of knowledge, but fools despise wisdom and instruction." The best place for wise counsel is the Bible. We must know God's Word and accept his instruction in order to make wise plans. Also, we get good advice when we commit our plans to the Lord in prayer. Proverbs 16:3 urges us to "Commit to the Lord whatever you do, and he will establish your plans." Second, it is important to know that once we make plans, God's will always prevails. We can take comfort in this once we know the character of God. In Jeremiah 29:11 we read, "For I know the plans I have for you," declares the Lord, "plans to prosper you and not to harm you, plans to give you a hope and a future."

A wise person accepts God's counsel and instruction then makes plans that align with God. By trusting in him and reading his Word, we will be wise through our later years and find peace in his plans instead of ours.

Carolyn Dun attends Christ Church Lake Forest. Carolyn serves the church as a member of the Mission Board and as a Financial Peace Coordinator. She has been a part of the church since 2002 when she started attending with her husband, Andrew, and two children who are now 21 and 23 years old. Her family lives in Lincolnshire and she recently formed a women's philanthropy group, Community Purse, with her Bible study friends.

BALANCE

By wisdom a house is built and through understanding
it is established. Through knowledge its rooms are
filled with rare and beautiful treasures.

Proverbs 24: 3-4

Earlier this year, Hank Smith and I joined a small team of North American churches to visit a team of believers serving the growing refugee community in Turkey. This trip was a vision trip—a chance to see the work being done in Turkey by one of Christ Church's mission partners. Our purpose was to try to understand how we could partner and serve those who are in great need—the oppressed and displaced migrants. Our hosts told us that we would meet men, women and children from Afghanistan, Iran, Iraq, Syria and African countries in conflict. I was intrigued and excited but I also felt that I needed wisdom—Godly wisdom—for this trip.

What would I say? How would I act? How could I respect and understand the cultural differences? What about all the people that watch the news and are concerned about our safety—what should I say to them? I want to serve well, but there is so much I don't understand. I needed help to think through this assignment. I needed guidance. I needed wisdom.

Biblical wisdom is the launching point. It is a place to seek instruction. To meditate on the Word of God, to pray and to truly understand all take time. How else can a person discover God's wise counsel? James 3:17 tells us that "wisdom that comes from heaven is first of all pure, then peace-loving, considerate, submissive, full of mercy and good fruit, impartial and sincere." Colossians 4:5-6 instructs us to be "wise in the way you act toward outsiders; make the most of every opportunity. Let your conversation always be full of grace... so that you may know how to answer everyone." These were good answers to my questions, good instruction.

Meditating on Scripture and being in prayer gives me solid footing and perspective on how to act and be culturally sensitive. It helps me be wise in relating to refugees, to be discerning in finding ways to serve and to be encouraging both to our fellow workers who've made Turkey their home and to the refugees in their ministry. Overall, meditating on Scriptures helps me trust God for safety.

While I have had the opportunity to travel to different countries, serve different churches, participate on mission trips and live in different cities, my understanding is incomplete without the instruction of God's Word. I can't rely too much on what I know. I shouldn't lean on my own understanding. Without meditating on his Word and seeking him in prayer, I am out of balance.

In Turkey, God showed me "rare and beautiful treasures"—people who found the love of Christ compelling and turned from their ways. We met a former jihadist from Egypt who is now a pastor. He asked us for forgiveness because of the prejudice he held against us as Americans. I was convicted of my own prejudices. We met a woman from a nomadic tribe in North Africa who gave powerful testimony to Jesus who saved her, forgave her and loves her. She now is pursuing a biblical education. She is trying to be obedient to God's calling to go and share the Good News with her family—a big task that will require godly wisdom.

What challenges are you facing that are bigger than you can handle today—challenges that require wisdom? Maybe it's not a trip to a place like Turkey or how to work with displaced and oppressed refugees. Maybe it's closer to home—your family, your spouse, your vocation, your volunteer work, your purpose, your future or a decision that needs to be made.

Whatever your circumstance, is your foundation secure? Are you relying on your own understanding—what you know and what you've seen? Pursue God in his Word—there is wisdom and insight available for all circumstances. As you read the Bible—give God your best time of day. Make time to be still and quiet before the Lord. He will meet you.

Mike Perkins attends Christ Church Crossroads. Mike serves the church as a deacon and on our Global Outreach Board. He has been a part of the church since 2007 when he started coming with wife, Betsy, and two children, a son who is 15 and a daughter who is 12. He and his family live in Libertyville.

WISE GUY

Remove the dross from the silver, and out comes material for the
silversmith; remove the wicked from the king's presence, and his throne
will be established through righteousness.

Proverbs 25:4-5

I played small college football and was blessed to have Scotty Kessler as my roommate. Kess was a two time All-American, captained our team and anchored our defense as a free safety. Beyond that, he was clearly the heart and soul of our team. During my junior year, we played for and won the National Championship in large measure due to Kess's leadership on and off the field.

We played for a legendary football coach who finished his career winning four National Championships. As tribute to Kess, our coach would often describe the timing, technique and sound of his bone-jarring tackles (often causing a fumble or interception) as something he could actually close his eyes and still hear.

God blessed Kess with good athletic ability and he did everything within his power to strengthen his body for the battle of a football season. He was physically strong, but his mental preparation was stronger still. He spent more time studying our opponents than any combination of players or coaches collectively; so much so that he'd repeatedly identify the slightest nuance in formation, cadence, or foot alignment to capitalize upon it for our team's benefit. As evidence of this, Kess shares the single game record for interceptions (four) in a National Championship football game.

Far beyond his athletic prowess, Kess was also our team's spiritual pacesetter. He would regularly say: "The horse is made ready for battle but victory rests in the Lord" (Proverbs 21:31), and encourage us by example to "be strong in the Lord and in his mighty power" (Ephesians 6:10).

Proverbs 25:4 states "Remove the dross from the silver, and out comes material for the silversmith." Scotty Kessler was a man constantly being made pure before God and giving himself in service to the Silversmith. This was true in preparing for football, preparing to lead young men on the field and especially true of the way he lived his adult life. Kess continues to be a lifelong learner resulting in favor with God and people and a reputation for good judgment.

This has come about from a diligent, wisdom-seeking pursuit of a daily relationship with God as well as a relentless commitment to ongoing dialogue with a set of trusted confidants.

Kess had a formula for wisdom living that came right from Jesus' own model:

- Jesus was always found getting away from distraction and seeking God

- Jesus engaged in significant loving relationships with a wide variety of people

Whatever impact Kess had on the playing field many years ago, it was nothing compared to the impact and influence of his life of faith. He loved God and loved others having a positive effect on literally thousands of others.

Garth Warren serves as the Campus Pastor at Christ Church Crossroads. He has been a part of the church since 2009 when he moved from Minnesota to join the staff as Executive Pastor. Garth and his wife, Kristy, love people and places and enjoy great relationships with their three adult children.

SMALL GROUP DISCUSSION
WEEK 4 : DEEP INSIGHT

The deep person knows how to arrange life purposefully in order to live in pursuit of spirit and truth. To live in pursuit of understanding and in relationship with God and His people. Insight is more than just acquiring a tip, it is the ability to recognize a whole new way and the willingness to give everything to find it.

LEANING:

What is some of the best advice you have ever received? Did you listen to it? Do you follow or use it still?

LEARNING:

Which proverb or devotion did you most connect with or feel inspired by this week? What did you like? What did you learn?

Proverbs 3:5-6 is a popular verse to quote. What would it look like to put this into action? Can you apply it to something you are facing right now? What would that mean for you?

LOVING:

What part of the sermon challenged you most or helped you grow perspective on God's love and wisdom?

Psalm 119 is broken into sections whose headings are the letters of the Hebrew alphabet (take a look now and you will understand). Pick a section and read it. What is the relationship of the psalmist to God and his Word in the section you read?

LIVING:

Have you ever tried Scripture memory? How might it be useful? (Psalm 119:11, Psalm 119:105)

Pick one of the Psalms between Psalm 120 and Psalm 131 and study it. Could you pray as the one writing/speaking the psalm does? How could this give you "voice" before God when you are praying and seeking him?

DIGGING DEEPER:

Review Acts 17. What is the difference between the Bereans (v. 11) and the Athenians (v. 21)? Which would you say you are more like? Would your spouse or best friend say the same thing? Why?

GRADUATE LEVEL:

Search the Gospels (Matthew, Mark, Luke and John) for times that "Jesus got away" (or something similar). What insight or strength was He seeking that prompted his retreats?

How might a retreat help you? Could it happen?

WEEK 5

DEEP INTIMACY:
FROM PROFANE
TO SACRED

If You Play With Fire | Proverbs 5

Look Beyond the Surface | Proverbs 11

Seduced | Proverbs 7

Recalibrating Our Hearts | Proverbs 23

That Woman | Proverbs 31

IF YOU PLAY WITH FIRE, YOU WILL GET BURNED

WARNING: Beware of the adulterous woman and pornography!
Although they may seem sweet, keep to a path far from them!
Do not go near! For if you do, you will lose your honor,
your dignity and your wealth.

Proverbs 5:3, 8-10 (paraphrase)

When my children turned a certain age, I took it upon myself to make sure they became aware of the facts of life, including the fact that they needed to be aware of those that might want to take advantage of them or lead them astray. I made sure to the best of my ability that my children were warned. On the topic of sexual temptation I told them, "decide in the light what you will do in the dark." On the topic of what they listened to and watched, I explained, "garbage in, garbage out." On the topic of pornography, I warned my son, "if you play with fire, you will get burned." I taught my girls how to effectively fight off unwanted advances. Apparently, I reminded them pretty frequently because they finally told me, "we know Mom—you don't need to tell us anymore." Okay—I might have overdone it a bit, but better safe than sorry, right? I took to heart what Proverbs warned in the way of temptation and sexual immorality.

In my own personal life I guarded my eyes, my heart, and my path. I honored my marriage vows and was "all in." I also watched over my children's activities. I knew God wanted the best for His children and gave us guidelines so that we could live the best possible life. I wanted to live the best possible life. I wanted my children to do the same. Life was going pretty well. My children made professions of faith and wisely chose friends who did the same. Every day I was thankful that "all was well." They left home, married believers and are now raising their children to follow the Lord. Whew! This was a Christian mother's dream come true. Someone even commented to me once that we were the "perfect Christian family."

But apparently not all was well on the home front. My husband was beginning to have issues at work. It wasn't really clear to me what these issues were, but he said it was "stressful." Then he started telling me stories from the office. A coworker, supposedly as a joke, put pornography on his computer screen. I was horrified and told him he needed to report it—I knew that if unreported and discovered, he could lose his job. Later, my husband came home upset that his laptop computer was taken and that he was moved from a private office to a public cubicle. Eventually, my husband was let go. The final discovery was that our home computer search history was filled with pornographic sites my husband had visited. When I approached him about this, his only response was "I'm not addicted." I connected him with a Christian counselor who specialized in sexual addictions, but my husband stopped going to counseling and then lied to me about it.

I have to admit that I was pretty naïve and trusting in my marriage. I didn't see this coming and the results of this form of sexual immorality have been devastating. Our family has experienced the impact of divorce. My ex-husband has experienced financial ruin and disgrace. He left the community he lived in nearly his entire life. Contact with his children and grandchildren is minimal. The pain is immense for us all. None of us wanted this—but this is now our reality. I have always preferred to learn from the mistakes of others and to heed warnings. It is my hope and intent that others will be able to learn and benefit from our story.

Be warned, when you play with fire, you (and all those around you) get burned.

Anonymous

LOOK BEYOND THE SURFACE

As a ring of gold in a swine's snout, so is
a beautiful woman who lacks discretion.

Proverbs 11:22

It was a Friday night in mid-September and I was an 18-year old college fresh-man at a school-sponsored dance looking to meet young women. Eventually, I found myself dancing with a pretty blonde named Annette. Over the flashing lights and loud music we danced for a few minutes, exchanged names, and moved on. We went our separate ways that evening, but I did not forget Annette. Her pretty face and engaging personality would not leave my thoughts. Over the course of the next two weeks, we somehow kept crossing paths—on campus, at a Christian retreat, studying in the library. I finally got around to asking her out for a cup of coffee. That was it. I was done for; head over heels in love. Three and a half years later we got married. After nearly twenty years of marriage and three children, that moment on the dance floor is a distant sweet memory.

In Proverbs 11:22, Solomon warns against chasing after a woman's beauty while ignoring her character and judgment. He compares it to becoming enamored with a golden ring, while disregarding the fact the ring is attached to the nose of a pig. Both men and women are often drawn to superficial outward appearances when it comes to attraction and love. We can easily fall in love with someone's looks, or sense of humor, their wit or even their money and possessions; while spending almost no effort to evaluate their character. As Solomon warns, you might fall in love with a golden ring and find yourself in a relationship with a pig.

I would love to be able to say I thoroughly evaluated Annette's character prior to our marriage. With almost four years of dating, I definitely was able to see many aspects of her character, but honestly I did not know what I was getting into. I really had no way of knowing that she would be such a devoted and loving mother to our children, or that she would be my source of encouragement and inspiration when life became difficult. There was no way for me to fully grasp the woman of God she would become, or her love for God's word and serving others. I thought I could never love her more than I did on the day we were married. I had no way of knowing how my love would grow deeper and stronger with every passing day. I had no way of knowing the blessing I was in for.

While God clearly blessed me with more than I deserved when I married Annette, it was based on more than good fortune. The foundation of our relationship has always been Jesus Christ. Our love and commitment has always been to Christ first and each other second. When I married Annette I was enamored with her beauty, but I knew I was not marrying a swine because she had built her life on the solid rock of Christ (Matthew 7:24-27). Love and marriage are arguably the most important decisions we make in life, after our decision to follow Christ. We need to regularly impart this Wisdom of Solomon to our children; and if we are single, heed it ourselves. To ignore this counsel is to risk a life of misery.

Ryan Harvey attends Christ Church Crossroads. Ryan currently sits on the Elder Board and enjoys serving in multiple capacities at the church. He has been a part of the church since 1997 when he started coming with his wife Annette, during which time they have been blessed with a girl and two boys ages 9, 11 and 13. His family lives in Libertyville and he loves to spend time in the mountains: trail running, fishing, hunting or hiking with his family.

SEDUCED

Soon she has him eating out of her hand, bewitched by honeyed speech.
Before you know it, he's trotting behind her, like a calf led to the butcher
shop, like a stag lured into ambush and then shot with an arrow, like a
bird flying into a net not knowing that its flying life is over.

Proverbs 7:21-23 (MSG)

Almost everywhere we look these days, there is a man or woman seductively looking back. Striking a pose. Inviting us into a fantasy world of some sort or another.

The most diligent adult cannot escape this reality, nor can our children be shielded from it. Several months ago, the most risqué version of the Sports Illustrated Swimsuit Edition was released. A friend called to tell of her pre-teen boys curiously exploring the cover, as it sat "innocently" amidst the children's and parenting magazines in the pediatrician's waiting room.

As a young child in the 1960s, I observed the neighborhood men's reactions to the then-popular Playboy magazine. Even at that tender age, it was clear to me that these women had a mesmerizing power over the men.

Seduction has always been with us, but in recent years, there has been tidal wave size growth in its prevalence—both in personal relationships and through widespread internet access to pornography, prostitution and sex trafficking.

Most people think, "It's no big deal."

I shared with my friend how media campaigns have dramatically changed our culture's perception of driving while drinking and of second hand smoke. "Maybe we could change the thinking on how we use each other's bodies?" I suggested. Her initial response, "Those other things are about life and death. This isn't."

Scripture says otherwise and the language from Proverbs is bone chilling. If we allow ourselves to be seduced, the Bible says we are being LED TO OUR GRAVE!

No shades of grey here.

If we toy with an adulterous affair, ease our stress with a dose of porn, or get our urges met through a prostitute, we are "like a stag lured into an ambush, then shot with an arrow." Or "like a bird flying into a net not knowing its flying life is over." We have become one of the many "victims brought down the highway to the grave, leading down to the chambers of death" (Proverbs 7:27).

I say this with no judgment. Seduction is wily. We don't have any idea as we are lured in step-by-step through "honeyed speech" or flattering looks, that it may *cost us our life*. Ultimately, we make a choice we thought we would never make, and that choice will lead "down to the chambers of death." The death will come in the form of losing the people we love, the respect of our community and the financial security we had, while gaining the weight of a web of secrets and lies, and a heavy burden of shame. This is where the real chamber of death is—in the shame.

Many years ago, I was seduced. And I stumbled and fell into this grave of shame, believing for a time that there was no way out. But, I was wrong. The good news is just as there is a highway that leads into the grave, there is a road that leads out as well. I have walked that road out hand-in-hand with Jesus. He graciously lit the path for my return and raised me from the dead into new life.

It breaks my heart when I see others languishing in the grave of shame, not understanding there is a way out. 1 John 1:9 says, "if we confess our sins, He will forgive us and He will purify us from all unrighteousness."

It breaks God's heart when we judge or condemn. We must align with the Word of God and know the truth. The one seduced is a victim. The seductress has typically been sexually abused herself. Most of the faces in porn and prostitution are modern day slaves, having been sadistically forced, coerced or manipulated into their trade.

Thankfully, our God is kind and compassionate, slow to anger and abounding in love. He sent Jesus into the world not to judge us, but to save us. May we let ourselves be saved; and then, join Jesus in rescuing other victims.

Suzanne Baker Brown has been part of the Christ Church of Lake Forest community since 2010. Suzanne has served the community as an intercessor, a Bible teacher for Spiritual Spa retreats, Women's Bible Connection, and the Care Ministry. She is the Executive Director of Stepping Stones Network, a not-for-profit addressing the issue of sex trafficking. She and her husband, Steve, live in downtown Chicago in the Uptown neighborhood.

RECALIBRATING OUR HEARTS

Give me your heart, my son, and let your eyes delight in my ways.
For a harlot is a deep pit, and an adulterous woman is a narrow well.
Surely she lurks as a robber, and increases the faithless among men.

Proverbs 23:26-28

When I was in high school and college, I could spend hours in a record store. I would lose myself in the credits on the backs of the album covers. "Glyn Johns produced The Rolling Stones' 'Sticky Fingers'?! Didn't he also produce The Who's album 'Who's Next'?" I would walk over to the "W" section to check it out. "Oh yeah, Shel Talmy produced 'My Generation.' No wonder that song sounds similar to 'You Really Got Me' by The Kinks." Then I would walk over to "K."

Music was my obsession. And after I came to Christ in my sophomore year at Miami of Ohio, it was a real distraction to any kind of spiritual growth. Rolling Stone magazine had been my Bible, and now it was competing with God's Word for my attention, and ultimately for my heart. I didn't start really growing in my new relationship with Christ until I actually laid music aside for a year and a half. No guitar playing, no secular music. In fact, I sold my 70's era Rickenbacker guitar for next to nothing, a decision I now deeply regret making! But I knew that if I was ever to use or enjoy music again, my view of it had to be reset. I needed to understand music from a completely different vantage point, as a gift from God intended as a blessing, to bring greater depth and enrichment to our lives. To view that gift properly, I needed to know the heart and ways of the One who designed it.

A year and a half after laying down music entirely, God made it clear to me that I was ready to pick it back up again. But my perspective toward all music had been realigned. It was viewed from the vantage point of a heart that delighted in God's ways and in His design. I'm not saying that the old distortion of the gift of music doesn't occasionally rear its head. But as long as my eyes are set on its

105

designer, I can enjoy it as it was designed to be enjoyed.

"Every good gift comes from the Father of Lights." But every good gift has a design, and when it is used outside of the context of that design, even a good thing like music can be a detriment, becoming an obsession, dislodging our balance and fracturing our wholeness as children of God. And when that good gift is as emotionally engaging and bonding as a sexual relationship, the distortion and fracturing can go to the core of our being.

The writer of Proverbs warns its reader to avoid pursuing sexual pleasure outside of the context that it was designed for. And the solution to those temptations is simple.

> Give me your heart, my son. And let your eyes delight in my ways.
> (Proverbs 23:26)

In another passage in Proverbs we're told to "guard your heart, for from it flow streams of life." If our loves and desires are misplaced, they will lead us toward distortion, imbalance, and a fractured soul.

The key to enjoying God's good gifts is a heart that belongs to the gifts' designer, and eyes that delight in His ways.

Brad Coleman is the Pastor of Worship for Christ Church. He leads worship in the sanctuary at the Lake Forest campus, and mentors the younger worship leaders in the other Christ Church worship venues. He has been a part of Christ Church since the summer of 2011 when he moved here from Southern California with his wife Margy and his twin daughters Addy and Ella. Brad is also a visual artist. He teaches a class at Lake Forest College in the art department, and does his own paintings whenever he can in the tiny attic of their home in Lake Forest.

THAT WOMAN I CAN NEVER LIVE UP TO

An excellent wife who can find? She is far more precious than jewels.
The heart of her husband trusts in her, and he will have no lack of gain.
She does him good, and not harm, all the days of her life.

Proverbs 31:10-12

We've all heard about her. In fact many of us have come to resent her. The perfect one. The one who set the standard so high the rest of us are doomed to fail by comparison. The one who is up before dawn everyday but continually has a smile on her face. The one who has a keen business sense, buying and selling commodities all day, but never lets anything fall through the cracks at home. The one who not only provides all the food and makes all the clothes for her family, but provides for the needs of others, as well. And most importantly, the one who always builds up her husband and never, ever disappoints him. Yep, this gal has certainly made it rough on the rest of us.

Proverbs 31:13-31 expounds even more on the many remarkable things she accomplishes. But when you strip away all the amazing "stuff" that she does, only one thing really matters. In verse 30, the Bible says, "Charm is deceitful, and beauty is vain, but a woman who fears the Lord is to be praised." Herein lies the secret. Her true worth comes not from what she does, but who she is in the Lord. Her countenance brims with confidence, strength, wisdom and grace that come from an obedient and submissive heart to God. That kind of inner beauty is more attractive than any designer clothes, extravagant jewelry, or expensive salon treatment. With her heart trusting fully in God alone, she is able to give freely and joyfully out of her overflow. And her husband is the chief recipient.

Okay. So instead of resenting her, let's ask ourselves how she is able to be and stay in that state of grace and peace with God. I am convinced, although the

Bible does not specifically say this, that she must have been a woman of prayer. No other activity in her day would even begin to match the enormous influence of this one simple act—coming before the God of the Universe and submitting each new day to Him, with all the pressures and temptations that it holds. Asking Him to do immeasurably more with it than she ever could on her own. And then trusting in God's goodness and sovereignty over her life, and praying for his blessing over those in her care.

And men, the lessons that we women take from this are not for us alone. We can all learn from this woman who fears the Lord above all else and whose whole life is marked by this devotion. We can all continually aspire to set aside the worldly influences and material things that compete for our time and our hearts.

"An excellent wife who can find?" In our present world of allure and distractions, this woman is a rare find. But I pray that God will find me faithfully seeking Him and, like her, count me as "far more precious than jewels."

Kristy Warren attends Christ Church Crossroads. Kristy serves the church as the volunteer women's coordinator at the Crossroads campus. She has been a part of the church since 2010 when she started coming with her husband, Garth. She has three children in their twenties and lives in Gurnee. Kristy enjoys reading, singing and taking long walks on the beach.

SMALL GROUP DISCUSSION
WEEK 5 : DEEP INTIMACY

Because the Deep person is a whole person, it is important to be able to discuss what deep means in the context of intimacy and sexuality. In many ways sexuality is being clouded and confused, and yet intimacy is still part of the identity of the person with inner depth. How do these ideas get combined in a meaningful way? (Suggestion for groups: This may be an opportunity to divide up by gender in order to have a more candid discussion.)

LEANING:

Is sexuality God's gift or Satan's trap?

LEARNING:

Which Proverbs or devotions did you most connect with or feel inspired by this week? What did you like? What did you learn?

What does intimacy mean? Is it exclusively a physical description?

LOVING:

What part of the sermon challenged you most or helped grow your perspective on God's love and wisdom?

Could a sexually supercharged world interfere with developing a healthy perspective of growing intimacy with God? Do you have suggestions how this could be untangled?

LIVING:

Consider Proverbs 6:20-7:27. What is the allure of the adulteress and adultery? What is the wisdom warning to help wisdom seekers counter the allure?

One of the devotions suggested this advice: "Decide in the light what you will do in the dark." What does this advice mean? Are there other practical ideas you can discuss to encourage one another to sexual purity?

DIGGING DEEPER:

Read 2 Samuel 11 and 12, 1 John 1:8-9, and Psalm 51. What led to David's sin? What could David have done differently? How complete was the restoration following Psalm 51? What did David do well? Is his circumstance and prayer relevant for people today?

GRADUATE LEVEL:

What are some of the places in Scripture where sexuality becomes problematic? Find 3-4 and share how God or God's people reacted? Do the collected stories broaden your understanding of God's heart? Do Jesus' experiences and interactions help reveal even more of God's heart?

DEEP BONDS:
FROM ISOLATION
TO CONNECTION

We Need Each Other | Proverbs 27

Taking the Right | Proverbs 12

A Mother's Loving Heart | Proverbs 21

Truth Wins Out | Proverbs 26

Prayer for Aslan | Proverbs 29

WE NEED EACH OTHER TO GO FROM DULL TO SHARP

As iron sharpens iron, so one person sharpens another.
The one who guards a fig tree will eat its fruit, and whoever
protects their master will be honored. As water reflects
the face, so one's life reflects the heart.

Proverbs 27:17-19

My husband and I were driving our '69 Chevy on the Hot Rod Power Tour and realized our numbers-only license plate didn't have much zing. So we emailed our kids with our problem, and they responded with CHEVOI, M T NEST, VELLE, VROOM, DOI TOY, KLNLVN and 69XQSES.

As iron sharpens iron, so one person sharpens another. We can choose to go from dull with no zing to iron-tough and iron-sharp.

We get tougher and sharper when we interact with other truth-seekers. Toughening comes from time invested with others who also are in God's fitness program. It doesn't happen through Facebook or Twitter because 140 characters are not enough to toughen us up.

So, where are these truth-seekers? Who is out there to get us ready to bring lethargic young adults back to church? Who will inspire us stand up for the persecuted? Who will help us understand the issues behind the sound bites? Who brings clarity to moral issues? Who will help me in my own faith journey?

And just when we're feeling totally helpless, we remember that we don't have the might or the power to do anything. But God does (Zechariah 4:6).

And God created us as relational beings to work with each other to spread his Word, feed the poor, heal the sick, comfort the widow and orphan—all through his powerful Spirit.

Remember Daniel? He was lifted out of his Judean home and culture and dumped into an alien one. How does one prepare for Babylon?

It's clear that Daniel had a good basic understanding of, and faith in, the one true God. And God was gracious enough to send along a team of three other iron-sharpening companions to help negotiate their pagan terrain in a God-honoring way. They could not have made it without a diet of God's three food groups: His Word, prayer and fearless faith that produces bold proclamation.

1. The Bible is truth. Eat it up (Ezekiel 3:1-2, Revelation 10:9-11). The one who tends the fig tree will eat its fruit and honor the Master. Drink deeply and you will reflect the One who has been teaching you (Proverbs 27:18-19).

2. Prayer. Especially with others. It's tough to be faithful in personal prayer, so the Lord encouraged us to join forces in prayer. Together we ask God to give us, forgive us, deliver us, lead us (Matthew 6:5-13). To gather together and pray. To lift our voices together to God (Acts 12:12).

3. Fearless faith reflects God in us. We can stand firm with truth and the iron sword of the Spirit, which is the word of God, praying at all times, so that we can declare boldly what we ought to speak (Act 4:24).

Some of us never have left home, yet we feel that Babylon has been dumped on our land. How do we negotiate this culture? Where do we find friends who can keep us sharp and God honoring? We could begin by seeking out the names at the bottom of these pages, and see if they want to engage in a little sword play.

Jean Doi attends Christ Church Lake Forest. Jean serves the church as a Bible teacher. She has been a part of the church for about 15 years when she started coming with her husband Jon. They live in Lake Bluff and have two grown children.

TAKING THE "RIGHT" OUT OF RIGHTEOUSNESS

*No harm overtakes the righteous, but the
wicked have their fill of trouble. The Lord detests lying lips,
but he delights in people who are trustworthy.*

Proverbs 12:21-22

For many people, the word "righteous" is hard to understand. When I was assigned this passage, I was a bit apprehensive. The first words that came to my mind are guilt, judgment and disappointment. The word righteous evokes beliefs about God and who I am in Christ. My false beliefs are rooted in fear and doubt; fears of unworthiness, being a disappointment, and never being able to do enough to please God.

When I committed my life to Christ I got the fresh start I needed. I was beyond excited! However, longing and living to win approval was a familiar path for me. So I brought an element of control into my faith by living and believing the more I did right, the more God would be pleased with me, and the more I could gain His love and acceptance. Every morning, I woke up early, read my Bible, and prayed for an hour. I led a women's Bible study outreach in my home. We sent our children to a Christian school and I led a moms' prayer group for many years. I truly believed what I understood at the time to be the "right" theology. I judged others by their marital struggles and how their kids seemed to be turning out. All the while, I was thinking, "Not *my* kids, not *my* husband, not *me*. We have it all figured out over here." I unknowingly covered my feelings of unworthiness with self-righteousness and superiority.

I believed I was one of the righteous and "no harm would come to me," just as God's word said.

Until the bottom of *my* world fell out.

All of a sudden, it seemed like God wasn't holding up his end of the deal.

I felt angry, discouraged and disillusioned. Really, God? This is what you do after all I've done?

I don't like the pruning process. I don't like the pain. I don't like the reflex answers that I often give about God wanting to stretch and grow me. What I do like, actually what I love, is how in the midst of my pain and process, my perception of God has grown and expanded from a God who is rigid and difficult to please, to a God who embraces me for who I really am.

> The Lord detests lying lips, but he delights in people who are trust-worthy. (Proverbs 12:22)

As I read verse 22, I imagine that God hates lying lips most of all, because lies are rooted in an inaccurate view of reality—who God is and who I am. I punish myself when I mess up; I answer other's requests based on what they have or have not done for me. He doesn't. I am starting to see how He wants me despite my failures, scars and imperfections. He wants my real, raw and authentic heart. I am beginning to taste and see the reality of God's grace as I become more willing to tell and accept the truth myself. As a result, I am finding more joy and freedom living life with Him.

When I live in the truth of who God is and the freedom of His grace, living a righteous life looks very different to me. Becoming righteous means more joy and delight in being who I am, facing the parts of me I don't like, and being with Him. This frees me to live from a heart filled with the desire to live in truth and love. To become more like Christ.

Sheryl Gould attends Christ Church Lake Forest. Sheryl serves the church as a One to One Ministry leader. She has been a part of the church since 2007 when she started coming with her husband, Todd, and three children who now range between 25 and 16. Her family lives in Lake Forest and Sheryl loves to support moms on the parenting journey.

A MOTHER'S LOVING HEART

The Righteous One observes the house of the wicked, he throws the wicked down to ruin. Whoever closes his ear to the cry of the poor will himself call out and not be answered.

Proverbs 21:12-13 (ESV)

Mommy! Mom! Mama! Mom! *Mommmyy!*

After waiting months for the boys to call me "Mama" instead of "Dada," I'll be honest and say there are days I wish I could change my name back to Dad. After over 40 hours a week alone with them, my name had been said, yelled, or whined hundreds, if not thousands of times, followed by requests for things ranging from food to help finding a specific Lego to breaking up an argument. Then there are the times it's shrieked out in the middle of the night, when I've been called upon to chase away imaginary rhinos, change sheets, or to rock one of the boys back to sleep. As their mom, I would never close my ears to my children. If they need me, no matter how busy or tired I am, I'll be there.

Yet, so often my relationships with God's other children don't cause me such an immediate response. I find myself focused on what *I* want or need. A car stopped on the side of the road can easily be looked over because *I'm* running late for an appointment. Someone short a few dollars in the check-out line at the grocery store can be ignored because *I'm* on a budget. A person struggling to open a door can be passed by because *my* hands are full. It's so easy to turn a deaf ear to those in need around me.

But Proverbs 21:21 tells us: "whoever pursues righteousness and kindness will find life, righteousness and honor."

It's easy to think that my appointment, my budget, or my full hands are the most important thing in the moment. But what is more important than life, righteousness and honor? In pursuing righteousness and kindness, I'm pursuing Christ himself.

I can often think of the "poor" as "those people over there with faraway needs in faraway lands," but in truth, anyone around me in need is the "poor." Daily, I can make the choice to have my ears open and to help. Just as I'd always turn toward my children, family, or friends in their time of need, I am called to turn toward the "poor."

It can be an overwhelming thought in a world full of people who all need something. But I trust each day that the people I'm supposed to help will be brought into my path. It's my job to keep my eyes open and my ears listening to the cries of those in need.

Kate Gleich attends Christ Church Crossroads. Kate served the church as the Coordinator of Mothers of Preschoolers (MOPS) for four years. She has been a part of the church since 2008 when she began attending with her husband, John. They now attend with their four boys, who range between a newborn and 6 years old. Her family lives in North Chicago and she loves making new friends.

TRUTH WINS OUT

Enemies disguise themselves with their lips, but in their hearts they harbor deceit. Though their speech is charming, do not believe them, for seven abominations fill their hearts. Their malice may be concealed by deception, but their wickedness will be exposed in the assembly.

Proverbs 26:24-26

In *The Lord of the Rings*, J.R.R. Tolkien provides a stark example of a wicked enemy disguised by charming speech. The Free Peoples (Men, Elves, Dwarves, and Hobbits), and various other creatures, including wizards, are locked in an epic struggle against the ultimate power of evil, who is trying to conquer the world and bring it into shadow. Wizards in Middle Earth are rare and powerful agents of good, somewhat similar to angels. They are possibly the most potent force standing against evil.

The leader of the wizards is Saruman the White. Tragically, Saruman is corrupted by the lure of power and falls to the evil side. Even after his fall, Saruman maintains the appearance of good. In addition, his voice is persuasive and powerful—he can sway nearly anyone with his charming speech. Gandalf (another wizard and a main character in the story) eventually discerns that Saruman is no longer on the side of good, but even he is deceived for some time. By the time Saruman's true nature is revealed, he has imprisoned the wise Gandalf and unleashed a ravaging army on his unsuspecting neighbors. In Proverbs 26, we read that wicked enemies often disguise themselves with their lips and speak in a charming manner. Saruman stands as a clear example of the warning in these verses: he deceives everyone around him with his words and appearance while he works his wicked schemes.

Most of us will never come into contact with as evil and powerful an enemy as Saruman, bent on domination and destruction, in our daily lives. Nonetheless, interpersonal relationships are replete with deception, either small or great.

Through direct lies or carefully chosen omissions, we shape the story we want others to believe about us. Many times our motives are driven by pride, fear, or selfishness. We take a "sick day" when really we just want a day off. We use our student ID to get discounts years after graduating. I have at times been deliberately vague about my age, driven by the misplaced desire to appear younger (full disclosure: I'm 42). More than once, when late to an appointment, I have told people I left earlier than I really did. I may not have been trying to con an enemy, or operating out of malice and wickedness, but this creates an untrustworthy foundation for relationships.

Proverbs 26 cautions us that what we see is not always what we get. People who intend harm may appear friendly and supportive for a time. I am reminded of Jesus' admonition to his disciples as he sent them out to preach, "I am sending you out like sheep among wolves. Therefore be as shrewd as snakes and as innocent as doves" (Matthew 10:16). Yet deception never lasts forever. Even as the true wickedness of Saruman was eventually revealed, so wickedness and deception will eventually "be exposed in the assembly" (Proverbs 26:26). Nonetheless, great harm can be done before this reveal occurs.

In God's economy, relationships are to be built on truth, honesty, and love. Rather than falling into patterns of deception to hide my true feelings or motivation, or to gain advantage or leverage over others, I should be known as a person of integrity. Examine your words and motives today and consider whether you have fallen into patterns of deception, whether small or large. What change can you make right now that will build your reputation as a man or woman of truth?

Matthew Heller attends Christ Church Crossroads. Matt serves the church as an elder, leader of the Bridge, and plays Joey in Route 6:6. He has been a member of the church since 2005. He and his wife Johanna have a daughter who will turn 1 in September. They live in Mundelein and keep one or two containers of homemade ice cream in the freezer at all times.

PRAYER FOR ASLAN

Discipline your son, and he will give you rest;
he will give delight to your heart.

Proverbs 29:17 (ESV)

I am an only child. To make matters worse, I am the only son of the eldest son. My father emigrated from Korea shortly after the Korean War, and was one of the first Korean exchange students. My grandfather, my father's father, a successful banker and entrepreneur had dreams of creating a new dynasty in the wealthiest country in the world. I learned at an early age that academic success, and entry to Harvard, would be the way to give my parents, my grandfather, our entire family, true happiness.

If I succeeded in this way, as Proverbs 29:17 promises, my family would have "rest" and "delight to their hearts." The "discipline" of hours of doing extra homework, piano practice, and SAT preparation would be my path.

The thin letter informing me of my rejection from Harvard was just the beginning of my struggle with feelings of failure—if only I had worked harder and been more disciplined.

I am now the father of an only son. AJ (whose first name is Aslan—yes, after the C.S. Lewis lion) is 11 years old. I have told him repeatedly that he needs to work harder and be more disciplined. AJ would most likely interject that the previous sentence is far from the truth. AJ's version which is closer to the truth than I would like to admit would be as follows: my father, in an uncontrollable rage, has screamed at me that I need to work harder and be more disciplined. AJ has described working on his Singapore math workbooks as human torture, and has recommended to his younger sister to choose a musical instrument that dad has not played.

Proverbs 29:17 does provide practical truth. For example, my mother shares with me her joy when she comes to AJ's violin recital and sees me accompanying him on the piano. She summarizes: The pain of discipline was well worth it.

If my mom's summary is God's primary instruction in Proverbs 29:17, having experienced it as a child as well as parent, I have a hard time believing that this is God's heart. Yes, we should discipline our children, but when we use our children as means to our happiness—our rest and peace—we sacrifice our children and use them as idols. I am guilty of this idolatry and still struggle with this idol, as AJ will attest.

My struggle with this idol however points me to my only hope, and also I believe points us to God's heart found in Proverbs 29:17.

I enjoy hugging AJ after having sought and received forgiveness from him when I have sinned against him. It reminds me of the Father hugging the Prodigal Son. It reminds me of Jesus hugging me.

Jesus alone can provide rest and peace to my heart.

I pray that I may discipline AJ by faith in Jesus. I pray that he would see it is not by his works or admittance to Harvard that he is loved, or saved, so that no one should boast. I pray that he would hug his child knowing that like his father he was saved by Grace.

Al Lee attends Christ Church Lake Forest. He serves the church as an Elder and Lighthouse Large Group Teacher. He has been a part of the church since 2007 when he started coming with his wife, Misun and two children, age 11 and 9. His family lives in Vernon Hills where Al hopes and prays AJ will turn from his ways as a St. Louis Cardinals fan and become a Cubs fan especially before next year, which is THE year that the Cubs will win the World Series.

SMALL GROUP DISCUSSION
WEEK 6 : DEEP BONDS

Our journey focused on loving God in order to become a person of inner strength—Deep. The reason to become Deep extends beyond living a well ordered life with God. The goal of love for God is transformation leading to love for God's people. The journey concludes with a focus on the value and deep bonds of being in God's community.

LEANING:

Excluding your current company (during the Small Group discussion), who are your closest friends? How did that relationship start? How did it grow?

LEARNING:

Which Proverbs or devotion did you most connect with or feel inspired by this week? What did you like? What did you learn?

How many "ingredients" that make a great relationship can you name? From your "brainstorm" can you prioritize five "ingredients" that you consider most important? How many of these do you bring to your closest friendships?

LOVING:

What part of the sermon challenged you most or helped grow your perspective on God's love and wisdom?

What is the core strength of healthy biblical community? After you have discussed, consider Acts 2:42-47?

LIVING:

Proverbs 17:17, Proverbs 18:24 and Proverbs 27:17 all speak to the value of friends. Has God used you to impact others in any of these ways? How else have you impacted others?

John 17:20-23 and Ephesians 4:1-17 speak of unity in the body of believers. What is so special or important about unity? How can it be achieved?

DIGGING DEEPER:

Watch Brené Brown's TED talk entitled "The Power of Vulnerability" online. It was the #4 talk of 1,600+ talks released. (The talk is about 20 minutes long—note: there is a bad word at 13:07.)

How do these popular ideas support God's vision for Biblical community? How does her insight simply reflect the truth of how God has always invited us to interact with each other?

GRADUATE LEVEL:

Jesus teaches that we should love our enemy and our neighbor. Cite some examples where Jesus or his disciples did this well. What can you learn from their interactions? What have you personally done in the last six months to love a neighbor or an enemy?

APPENDIX

HOST TRAINING

Congratulations! You have responded to the call to help shepherd Jesus' flock. There are few other tasks in the family of God that surpass the contribution you will be making. As you prepare to lead, whether it is one session or the entire series, here are a few thoughts to keep in mind. We encourage you to read these and review them with each new discussion leader before he or she leads.

1. **Remember that you are not alone.** God knows everything about you, and He knew that you would be asked to lead your group. Remember that it is common for all good leaders to feel they are not ready to lead. Moses, Solomon, Jeremiah and Timothy—they all were reluctant to lead. God promises, "never will I leave you; never will I forsake you" (Hebrews 13:5). Whether you are leading for one evening, for several weeks, or for a lifetime, you will be blessed as you serve.

2. **Don't try to do it alone.** Pray right now for God to help you build a healthy leadership team. If you can enlist a co-leader to help you lead the group, you may find your experience to be much richer. This is your chance to involve as many people as you can in building a healthy group. All you have to do is call and ask people to help. You'll be surprised at the response.

3. **Just be yourself.** If you won't be you, who will? God wants you to use your unique gifts and temperament. Don't try to do things exactly like another leader—do them in a way that fits you! Just admit it when you don't have an answer and apologize when you make a mistake. Your group will love you for it, and you'll sleep better at night!

4. **Prepare for your meeting ahead of time.** Listen to the sermon, read the devotions and associated Proverbs, then review the small group session and write down your responses to each question. Pay special attention to exercises that ask group members to do something other than engage in discussion. These exercises will help your group live what the Bible teaches, not just talk about it. Be sure you understand how an exercise works, and bring any necessary supplies (such as paper and pens) to your meeting.

5. **Pray for your group members by name.** Before you begin your session, go around the room in your mind and pray for each member by name. You may want to review the prayer list at least once a week. Ask God to use your time together to touch the heart of every person uniquely. Expect God to lead you to whomever he wants you to encourage or challenge in a special way. If you listen, God will surely lead!

6. **When you ask a question, be patient.** Someone will eventually respond. Sometimes people need a moment or two of silence to think about the question, and if silence doesn't bother you, it won't bother anyone else. After someone responds, affirm the response with a simple "thanks" or "good job." Then ask, "How about somebody else?" or "Would someone who hasn't shared like to add anything?" Be sensitive to new people or reluctant members who aren't ready to say, pray or do anything. If you give them a safe setting, they will blossom over time.

7. **Break up into small groups each week, or they won't stay.** If your group has more than eight individuals or six couples, we strongly encourage you to have the group gather in discussion circles of four to six people during the LOVING or LIVING sections of the study. With a greater opportunity to talk in a small circle, people will connect more with the study, apply more quickly what they're learning and ultimately get more out of it. A small circle also encourages a quiet person to participate and tends to minimize the effects of a more vocal or dominant member. This will help people feel more loved and important in the group. When you gather again at the end of the discussion, someone can summarize for each group. Finally, the small circles also help for prayer time. This helps people who normally don't pray aloud, since there are only four or five others. Also prayer requests won't take as long, leaving more time to actually pray. If you do this, make sure that someone reports back to the whole group about the prayer requests of your circle. This way, the whole group is not missing out on what happens in the subgroups.

8. **Rotate facilitators.** At some point you might end a meeting and ask the group who could lead the following week. Let the group help select your facilitator. You may be perfectly capable of leading each time, but you will help others grow in their faith and gifts if you give them opportunities to lead. You can use the Small Group Calendar to fill in the names of leaders for all your meetings at once if you prefer.

9. **One final challenge (for new or first time leaders):** Before your first opportunity to lead, look up each of the five passages listed below. Read each one as a devotional exercise to help equip you with a shepherd's heart. If you do this, you will be more than ready for your first meeting.

Matthew 9:36
1 Peter 5:2-4
Psalm 23
Ezekiel 34:11-16
1 Thessalonians 2:7-8, 11-12

HOSTING FOR THE FIRST TIME

- **Sweaty palms are a healthy sign.** The Bible says God is gracious to the humble. Remember who is in control; the time to worry is when you're not worried. Those who are soft in heart (and sweaty palmed) are those whom God is sure to speak through.

- **Seek support.** Ask your leader, co-leader or close friend to pray for you and prepare with you before the session. Walking through the study will help you anticipate potentially difficult questions and discussion topics.

- **Bring your uniqueness to the study.** Lean into who you are and how God wants you to uniquely lead the study.

- **Prepare. Prepare. Prepare.** Go through the session several times. Watch the teaching segment and SmallTALK Videos. Consider writing in a journal or fasting for a day to prepare you for what God wants to do.

- **Ask for feedback so you can grow.** Perhaps in an e-mail or on cards handed out at the study, have everyone write down three things you did well and one thing you could improve on. Don't get defensive, but show an openness to learn and grow.

- **Prayerfully consider launching a new group.** This doesn't need to happen overnight, but God's heart is for this to happen over time. Not all Christians are called to be leaders or teachers, but we are all called to be "shepherds" of a few.

- **Share with your group what God is doing in your heart.** God is searching for those whose hearts are fully His. Share your trials and victories. We promise that people will relate.

- **Prayerfully consider to whom you would like to pass the baton next week.** It's only fair. God is ready for the next member of your group to go on the faith journey you just traveled.

SMALL GROUP AGREEMENT

Our Purpose:

To transform our spiritual lives by cultivating our spiritual health in a small group community.

We do this through:

Group Attendance	To give priority to the group meeting. We will call or email if we will be late or absent. (Completing the Group Calendar will minimize this issue.)
Safe Environment	To help create a safe place where people can be heard and feel loved. (Please, no quick answers, snap judgments or simple fixes.)
Respect Differences	To be gentle and gracious to people with different spiritual maturity, personal opinions, temperaments or imperfections. We are all works in progress.
Confidentiality	To keep anything that is shared strictly confidential and within the group; and to avoid sharing improper information about those outside the group.
Encouragement for Growth	To be not just takers but givers of life. We want to spiritually multiply our life by serving others with our God-given gifts.
Welcoming Newcomers	To keep an open chair and share Jesus' dream of finding a shepherd for every sheep.
Shared Ownership	To remember that every member has a ministry and to ensure that each attender will share a small team role or responsibility over time.
Rotating Hosts/Leaders and Homes	To encourage different people to host the group in their homes and to rotate the responsibility of facilitating each meeting. (See the Group Calendar)

Extras to consider for agreement:
- ☐ Child Care
- ☐ Refreshments/mealtimes
- ☐ When we will meet (day)
- ☐ Where we will meet (place)
- ☐ When we will begin (time)

SMALL GROUP CALENDAR

Planning and calendaring can help ensure the greatest participation at every meeting. At the end of each meeting, review this calendar. Be sure to include a regular rotation of host homes and leaders, and don't forget birthdays, socials, church events, holidays or any service projects you might recognize or celebrate together.

DATE	LESSON	HOST NAME

DESSERT/MEAL/SNACK	LEADER

SMALL GROUP ROSTER

Taking the time on the first night to fill out the small group roster will give you all a chance to review the names on the list and be better prepared to use names the next week. Additionally, having contact information in a handy place will facilitate contacting each other and building relationships with one another.

NAME	ADDRESS

PHONE	EMAIL

NOTES

NOTES

NOTES

NOTES

NOTES

NOTES

NOTES